The CSS H. L. Hunley

Confederate Submarine

By

R. Thomas Campbell

 BURD STREET PRESS

This Burd Street Press publication
was printed by
Beidel Printing House, Inc.
63 West Burd Street
Shippensburg, PA 17257-0152 USA

In respect for the scholarship contained herein, the acid-free paper used in this book meets the guidelines for permanence and durability of the Committee on Production Guidelines for Book Longevity of the Council on Library Resources.

For a complete list of available publications
please write
Burd Street Press
Division of White Mane Publishing Company, Inc.
P.O. Box 152
Shippensburg, PA 17257-0152 USA

Library of Congress Cataloging-in-Publication Data

Campbell, R. Thomas, 1937-
    The CSS *H.L. Hunley* : Confederate submarine / by R. Thomas Campbell.
        p. cm.
    Includes bibliographical references and index.
    ISBN 1-57249-175-2 (alk. paper)
    1. H.L. Hunley (Submarine) 2. Confederate States of America. Navy--History. 3. Submarines (Ships)--United States--History--19th century. 4. Charleston (S.C.)--History--Civil War, 1861-1865. 5. United States--History--Civil War, 1861-1865--Naval operations--Submarine. I. Title.
    E599.H4 C36   1999
    973.7'57--dc21   99-35335
                                                                      CIP

PRINTED IN THE UNITED STATES OF AMERICA

To the memory of Lieutenant George E. Dixon,
last commander of the Confederate submarine
CSS *H. L. Hunley*, these pages are humbly dedicated.

Contents

Illustrations

Acknowledgments

I would like to thank the many persons and institutions that aided in the compilation of these few pages. These include Mark K. Ragan and Daniel Dowdey, both of whom have been very helpful. In addition, Chris Amer of the South Carolina Institute of Archaeology and Anthropology, and Dr. E. Lee Spence provided many interesting details on the discovery of the *Hunley*.

Others include the Civil War Library and Museum of Philadelphia, the U.S. Army War College at Carlisle, Pennsylvania, the Museum of the Confederacy in Richmond, Virginia, and last but not least, my wife, Carole. Without her encouragement, patience, and editing expertise, this work would not have been possible.

Introduction

Some of the interested citizens of Charleston, South Carolina may have become accustomed to the sight; others, however, had not. Charleston harbor was alive with naval activity, and the sight of ungainly ironclads and cigar-shaped torpedo boats had become common. But this vessel defied description. Visible from the waterfront and the "Battery" almost every evening during the approaching winter of 1863 was the long, low shape of a peculiar looking vessel. It usually rested with its blackened iron hull barely awash in the rippling harbor waters. Usually near sundown, observers would notice nine men, two of them officers, clamber onto the craft and disappear into its interior. A lone sailor, standing in an open hatchway, would cast off the lines and then he, too, would vanish below. Slowly, the strange craft would ease into the channel and begin to make its way out of the anchorage. With no protruding sail or smokestack, its upper surface was barely visible above the water. Two squat towers, one forward and one aft, were all that interrupted the sleek lines of the black silhouette. Gently rising and falling with the swells of the outgoing tide, the mysterious vessel glided silently out toward the cold green waters of the Atlantic Ocean. Occasionally, as the boat would rise on an unusually large swell, a long spar could be discerned protruding from the bow with a sinister-looking black cylinder attached to the far end.

As the bizarre craft proceeded out in the direction of the Federal blockading fleet, perceptive viewers, perhaps with a high quality telescope, could see the hatch covers close, then suddenly, in a surge of bubbles, the boat would disappear beneath the surface. At that point, some may have turned away sadly or started for home thinking another boat had sunk in the harbor and more wives and mothers would be crying by morning. But if they lingered long enough, perhaps twenty minutes or more, and there was still enough light, they might have caught a distant glimpse farther down the channel. Silently, it would break the surface briefly, only to sink again and be lost from view in the gathering darkness. Strangely enough, early daylight usually found the vessel tied to the dock where it would be rocking gently in the wake of the morning boats passing by. Several times, however, it had not returned, at least not by its own power. On those occasions, it took several days for divers to locate the sunken craft. When finally raised by cranes from the bottom, and the hatches opened, a sad and gruesome sight greeted those nearby. It was plainly evident that her crew had died a desperate and terrifying death.

In spite of these failures, little did the residents of the city realize that they were historic witnesses to what would become the world's first successful submarine. Forerunner of all the great and fearsome undersea craft to come in a later century, this historic vessel that they were watching was the Confederate submarine, CSS *H. L. Hunley*. No other vessel built by or for the Confederacy is as intriguing and innovative as the *Hunley*. Even the swift cruisers such as *Alabama* or *Shenandoah*, the mighty ironclads like *Virginia*, *Arkansas*, or *Tennessee* cannot rival the little *Hunley* for its sheer genius in concept, construction, and operation.

The Southern volunteers who crewed this small submarine, and lost their lives in doing so, were entering a realm that few in the nineteenth century could conceive or understand. It required extraordinary courage to enter this realm. On at least two occasions, when the *Hunley* was lost and the crew suffocated, Confederate Navy volunteers had stepped forward to form a new crew even before the craft was salvaged from the ocean floor. They knew only too well that if the sub ran into trouble while submerged that there was no way to replenish the air supply. They could do little but await the inevitable end.

A single candle by the commander's side at the forward end of the boat provided the only illumination. The light barely penetrated to those unfortunate sailors sweating at the propeller crank in the rear. When the flickering light went out due to the lack of oxygen, it became a stark reminder to all of just how close they were to suffocation. Working now in total darkness, they placed their trust and their lives in the hands of the man at the forward diving-planes.

As they sought out their country's enemy, the farthest thought from their minds was the fact that they were introducing a whole new concept and dimension to naval warfare. A concept and dimension that is embodied in the huge nuclear-powered, missile-firing submarines of today. But as history has recorded, it was these Southern heroes who led the way.

This, in brief, is the story of those dedicated men and the fascinating machine they took into battle.

Chapter One
The Pioneer

The *Hunley* may have found its moment of glory at Charleston, but its ancestry began in New Orleans, Louisiana, and its lineage can be traced to the very beginning of the War Between the States. When the Southern states chose to sever their ties with the American union, they hoped for a peaceful separation. Whether that separation would be peaceful or not, the South was eager and determined to become an independent nation.

Many in the North were resigned to allow their Southern brethren to depart in peace, but one, President Abraham Lincoln, was not. The newly elected president was inflexible in his resolve to preserve the Union and he would utilize force if need be to achieve that objective. On April 12, 1861, having learned that reinforcements were on the way, Confederate guns in Charleston, South Carolina opened fire on Fort Sumter. Two days later Lincoln issued a call for 75,000 volunteers to "suppress the rebellion." The War Between the States had begun.

One of the first objectives of the Lincoln government was to devise a mechanism for cutting off the importation of supplies and munitions from overseas to the Southern states. Lincoln's cabinet advised him not to use the term "blockade" in his April 19 proclamation, for international law indicated that this term would bestow legitimacy upon the Confederacy and entitle it to recognition by foreign governments.

They pointed out that a country could effectively close its own ports through passage and enforcement of tax laws, but that a blockade was defined as an act of war that was only recognized as legal when used against an enemy nation. Lincoln ignored his advisors, however, and declared a formal blockade of the Southern coast.

While eager volunteers swelled the ranks of the Southern armies, the newly created Confederate Navy was desperately searching for almost anything that would float. In spite of the need for warships to counter the Federal Navy, few in the South believed that the blockade could ever truly become effective. With thirty-five hundred miles of coast line it would be impossible for the North to patrol it all. In a few months, however, the frowning masts of enemy warships began to appear off Southern ports.

With no navy to speak of at this time, something had to be done to counter this growing naval threat. By late spring of 1861 the Confederate Congress had passed a bill authorizing the government to issue commissions to private citizens who wished to act as privateers. Southern leaders believed that the only hope of ultimate victory rested in breaking the blockade that was beginning to cut them off from badly needed European munitions and supplies. By mid-nineteenth century, most governments had outlawed the practice of privateering on the high seas. Desperate times called for bold measures, however. All over the South, groups and individuals who had fabricated anything from iron rams to floating gun batteries submitted applications for letters of marque and reprisal.

The United States government never publicly recognized Southern privateers as anything but pirates, for to do so would have conveyed the connotation that the United States recognized the Confederacy as a belligerent nation. Throughout the war, the Northern government maintained this position, denying any legitimacy to the existence of the Confederate States. To have done otherwise would have revealed that the invasion and subjugation of the Southern states was nothing more than open aggression. In Europe the Confederacy was recognized as a belligerent and was granted all the rights and privileges that international law provided. Although Great Britain, France, Austria, Prussia, Russia, Sardinia, and Turkey had taken steps to abolish privateering at the Treaty of Paris in 1856, the United States had never become a signatory to the treaty. In no way then, were the former states of the Union, which now formed the Confederacy, bound by the Treaty of Paris. While Lincoln and Secretary of State William Seward fumed about the Southern "pirates," every nation of the world recognized the legitimate right of the "de facto" government in Montgomery to issue letters of marque and reprisal.

President Davis' proclamation stated:

Whereas Abraham Lincoln, the President of the United States, has by proclamation announced the intention of invading this Confederacy with an armed force for the purpose of capturing its fortresses and thereby subverting its independence and subjecting the free people thereof to the dominion of a foreign power; and

Whereas it has thus become the duty of this Government to repel the threatened invasion and to defend the rights and liberties of the people by all the means which the laws of nations and the usages of civilized warfare place at its disposal:

Now, therefore, I, Jefferson Davis, President of the Confederate States of America, do issue this my proclamation inviting all those who desire, by service in private armed vessels on the high seas, to aid this Government in resisting so wanton and wicked an aggression, to make application for commissions or letters of marque and reprisal to be issued under the seal of the Confederate States.

Jefferson Davis, April 17, 1861.[1]

The idea of using privately owned and armed vessels to wage war on the commerce of one's enemy is as old as naval warfare itself. The French were the first to send out these private raiders of the sea on a large scale. During the Seven Years War, French privateers made several thousand prizes. Private vessels, sanctioned by the government of King Louis XV, destroyed more than eight hundred British trading vessels when there was scarcely a French ship-of-the-line left to fight the British. During the American Revolution and the War of 1812, American attacks on British commerce were carried on almost exclusively by these privately armed raiders.

Privateering provided a means for a weaker nation to strike a blow at an enemy's commerce, without having to build its own strong naval force. The incentive for private citizens to arm their vessels and attempt to capture the vessels of their country's enemy, of course, was profit—hopefully, patriotism and profit. Rules set down in the granting of a letter of marque and reprisal, required that vessels captured by a privateer be sailed to the nearest port of the privateer's origin, where the prize was to be adjudicated by a court of law. If the prize was condemned, meaning the vessel and its cargo were found to be the property of the enemy, the ship and its cargo were sold to the highest bidder with the owners, officers, and crew of the privateer dividing the proceeds.[2]

J. Thomas Scharf, who was a Confederate midshipman during the war, described very accurately the nature of a privateer:

"A privateer, as the name implies, is a private armed ship, fitted out at the owner's expense, but commissioned by a belligerent government to capture the ships and goods of the enemy at sea, or the ships of neutrals when conveying to the enemy goods [that are] contraband of war. A privateer differs from a pirate in this, that one has a commission and the other has none. A privateer is entitled to the same rights of war as the public vessels of the belligerent. A pirate ship has no rights, and her crew are liable to be captured and put to death by all nations as robbers and murderers on the high seas. The policy of neutrals recognizing privateers as legitimate belligerent ships is founded on the interest of humanity and the common desire to prevent piracy. If privateers were not recognized by neutral nations they would become pirates, and instead of making prisoners of the crews of the prize vessels, they would massacre them, appropriate the cargoes and sink the ships. But, being recognized, they are under the surveillance of the government commissioning them as well as the governments of neutral nations, and they are responsible for their acts to both."[3]

Although President Davis had issued his proclamation, he refrained from issuing any letters of marque until his decision could be approved by the House of Representatives and the Senate. On May 6, 1861, the Confederate Congress passed an act recognizing the existence of a state of war between the Confederate States and the United States. Section one of this act stated:

> The Congress of the Confederate States of America do enact, that the President of the Confederate States is hereby authorized to use the whole land and naval force of the Confederate States to meet the war thus commenced, and to issue to private-armed vessels commissions, or letters of marque and general reprisal, in such form as he shall think proper....[4]

During this hectic period of mobilization, an interesting letter appeared in the *Columbia Herald*, a newspaper published in Columbia, Tennessee. It was reprinted in several other newspapers throughout the Southern states. Written by an inventor named Frances Smith, the article was dated June 10, 1861:

"From the Chesapeake to the mouth of the Rio Grande, our coast is better fitted for submarine warfare than any other in the world. I would have every hostile keel chased from our coast by submarine propellers. The new vessel must be cigar shaped for speed, made of plate iron, joined without external rivet head; about 30 feet long, with a central section about 4 x 3 feet driven by a spiral propeller. The new Aneroid Barometer made for increased pressure, will enable the adventurer easily to decide his exact distance below the surface....I am preparing a detailed memoir on submarine warfare, discussing matters not proper to be spoken of here, illustrated with engravings. Copies of the pamphlet will be sent to the mayors and municipal authorities of

Southern maritime cities. Applications from independent individuals must be made through the local authorities."[5]

A copy of this article may well have found its way into the small New Orleans machine shop of James McClintock and Baxter Watson. The two men for some time before the outbreak of hostilities had been engaged in the fabrication of steam gauges and miscellaneous parts for steam engines. Devoted to the Southern cause, the two partners by the autumn of 1861 had designed and sold two bullet-making machines to the Confederate government. With offers of letters of marque from the president, and perhaps with the newspaper article in mind, the two began the construction of a radically conceived submersible boat which was intended to become a privateer.

This first venture was fabricated in the Leeds foundry, on the corner of Fourcher and Delord Streets, not far from their own shop. The craft was constructed from ¼-inch iron sheets bolted to an iron frame. The bolt heads were hammered flush and a small spiral propeller which was turned by hand from the inside was fitted. Diving planes on either side and actuated by a lever from within controlled descent and ascent. Many of the features designed into this first venture, which would eventually come to be named *Pioneer*, were embodied in later underseas craft including the *Hunley*.[6]

At some time during the construction of this first submersible at the Leeds foundry, another man whose name would forever be linked with the world's first successful submarine, invested $400 of his own money in the project. His name was Horace Lawson Hunley of New Orleans. At the time he was the deputy collector of customs in the Crescent City, in addition to being a wealthy planter and practicing attorney. Originally from Sumner County, Tennessee, where he was born on December 29, 1823, Hunley's family moved to New Orleans when the young lad was only eight years old. Educated at the University of Louisiana (now Tulane), the young Hunley had compiled many notable achievements in the years prior to the war.[7]

Devoted to the Southern cause, Hunley realized early in the conflict that the key to Confederate success was in keeping the supply lines open between Europe and the Southern states. In June of 1861, he traveled to Cuba to obtain arms and to plot a safe route for the transshipment of supplies. In a letter to the Confederate Secretary of War, a colleague of Hunley's wrote: "The report of H. L. Hunley who had charge of the expedition will be valuable in transferring arms and munitions to the Confederate States."[8]

In addition to McClintock, Watson, and Hunley, three other investors came forward to help finance the building of the submersible taking shape in the Leeds foundry: custom house employer and diver John K. Scott, Hunley's wealthy brother-in-law Robert Ruffin Barrow, and prominent lawyer and newspaper editor Henry J. Leovy. These six men constituted the driving force behind the construction of the *Pioneer*.[9]

In early February 1862, the completed *Pioneer*, most likely covered by a tarpaulin for security, was loaded and chocked on a wagon bed and hauled to the New Basin dock. Only the builders, owners, and a few select members of the military were on hand to witness the first trials. To the amazement of the military skeptics, the small submarine proved quite seaworthy, requiring only minor modifications to stop the leaks that seeped in around her seams. Towed down the canal to Lake Pontchartrain, the three-man submarine, under the command of Scott, proved to be exceptionally controllable within the calm waters of the lake. Writing to Commander Matthew Maury after the war, McClintock described these early tests:

"In the years 1861, 62, and 63, I, in connection with others, was engaged in inventing and constructing a submarine boat or boat for running under the water at any required depth from the surface. At New Orleans in 1862 we built the first boat, she was made of iron ¼ inch thick. The boat was of a cigar shape 30 feet long and 4 feet in diameter, with a propeller in one end, turned with a crank by two persons inside the boat. This boat demonstrated to us the fact that we could construct a boat that would move at will in any direction desired, and at any distance from the surface. As we were unable to see objects after passing under the water, the boat was steered by a compass, which at times acted so slow, that the boat would at times alter her course for one or two minutes before it would be discovered, thus losing the direct course and so compel the operator to come to the top of the water more frequently than he otherwise would."[10]

According to McClintock, during these trials with Scott at the controls, the *Pioneer* was able to destroy a schooner and two target barges. Satisfied with the results of the tests in Lake Pontchartrain, the submarine was towed back to the New Basin dock and a letter of marque and reprisal was applied for. The letter to the authorities in Richmond stated:

New Orleans, March 12, 1862.

Hon. J. P. Benjamin,
Secretary of State, Richmond, Va.

Sir: Application is hereby made for a commission or authority in the name of the Government of these States, to issue to the undersigned as commander of the submarine boat called the *Pioneer* for authority to cruise the high seas, bays, rivers, estuaries, etc., in the name of the Government, and aid said Government by the destruction or capture of any and all vessels opposed to or at war with said Confederate States, and to aid in repelling its enemies.

Said vessel is commanded by John K. Scott, who is a citizen of New Orleans and of this Confederacy. Said vessel was built at New Orleans in the year 1862; is a propeller; is 34 feet in length; is 4 feet breadth; is 4 feet deep. She measures about 4 tons; has round conical ends and is painted black. She is owned by Robert R. Barrow, Baxter Watson, and James R. McClintock, all of this city of New Orleans. She will carry a magazine of explosive matter, and will be manned by two men or more.

And I hereby promise to be vigilant and zealous in employing said vessel for the purpose aforesaid and abide by all laws and instructions and at all times acknowledge the authority of the Government of said States and its lawful agent and officers.

Considering his bond the undersigned prays for the issurance of a commission or letter of marque.

John K. Scott.[11]

According to the register of commissions issued to applicants for letters of marque on file at the New Orleans Custom House, John Scott was issued a commission for the *Pioneer* on March 31, 1862. The commission was secured by a $5,000 bond which listed the sureties as Horace L. Hunley and Henry J. Leovy.

With the commission as a privateer in hand, Scott and his two-man crew were no doubt eager to place their submarine in a position where one or two of the enemy vessels gathered outside New Orleans could be attacked. A lucrative bounty could be anticipated for every enemy vessel they might destroy. But the little *Pioneer* never had an opportunity to meet the enemy, for on April 24, Captain David G. Farragut's armada of warships fought their way past Forts Jackson and St. Philip at the mouth of the Mississippi River. Sweeping aside the determined but overwhelmed Confederate naval resistance, Farragut's fleet steamed upriver toward New Orleans.

With the collapse of Confederate defenses and the capture of the city imminent, retreating Southern troops burned and destroyed anything and everything that could be useful to the victorious Union forces. One Federal officer wrote that: "The river and shore were one blaze, and the sounds of explosions were terrific."[12] Smoke from thousands of bales of burning cotton filled the air, and the streets were filled with frightened citizens struggling to make their way out of the city. Hunley, Watson, and McClintock quickly scuttled the *Pioneer* in the New Basin Canal. Hurrying back to their shop at 31 Front Levee, the three men gathered their drawings, diagrams, and notes and joined the mob of refugees clogging the roads leading out of New Orleans. With all their possessions lost, save what they could carry, the disappointed trio headed for Mobile, Alabama, where they hoped to build a larger and more formidable submarine boat.

With the occupation of New Orleans, Union sailors discovered the sunken *Pioneer* and had it dragged up on shore. Intrigued by the contraption and concerned about future threats from such boats, the Federal authorities dispatched G. W. Beard, a young engineer's assistant, to inspect the boat. Writing after the war, Beard gives us a fascinating, but brief, glimpse of this early predecessor to the *Hunley*:

"When a third assistant aboard the *Pensacola* during the Civil War, I had the pleasure of assisting Second Assistant Engineer Alfred Colin in the measurements and drawings of a submarine torpedo boat which had been fished out of the canal near the 'New Basin' between New Orleans and Lake Pontchartrain. Mr. Colin's drawing was sent by the Fleet Engineer (Mr. Shock) to the Navy Department."

"The boat was built of iron cut from old boilers, and was designed and built by Mr. McClintock, in his machine shop in the city of New Orleans. She was thirty feet in length; the middle body was cylindrical, ten feet long, and the ends were conical. She had a little conning tower with a manhole in the top, and small, circular, glass windows in its sides. She was propelled by a screw, which was operated by one man. She had vanes, the functions of which were those of the pectoral fins of a fish. The torpedo was of a clockwork type, and was intended to be screwed into the bottom of the enemy's ship. It was carried on top of the boat, and the screws employed were gimlet-pointed and tempered steel.

Mr. McClintock (whom I met after the Civil War had ended) informed me that he had made several descents in his boat, in the lake, and succeeded in destroying a small schooner and several rafts. He stated that the U.S. Steamers *New London* and *Calhoun* had been a menace on the lake, and this gave rise to the torpedo boat; but before an attack was made the fleet of Farragut had captured New Orleans, and his boat was sunk to prevent her from falling into the hands of the enemy."[13]

The history of Confederate submarine boats at New Orleans was not about to end there. Some early post-war writers claimed that the *Pioneer's* operations came to an abrupt end when the craft became unmanageable and sank taking the crew with it. This, however, appears not to have been the case. In McClintock's letter to Matthew Maury, he states that: "The evacuation of New Orleans lost this boat before our experiments were completed...." William Alexander, who later would become closely associated with the *Pioneer's* successor, the CSS *Hunley*, sheds more light on the fate of the boat:

"Shortly before the capture of New Orleans by the United States troops, Captain Hunley, Captain James McClintock, and Baxter Watson were engaged in building a submarine torpedo-boat in the New Basin of that city. The city falling into the hands of the Federals before it was completed, the boat was sunk and these gentlemen came to Mobile."[14]

On February 15, 1868, an article appeared in the New Orleans *Picayune*:

AUCTION SALES.

A torpedo boat, which was built in this city or hereabouts during the war, and which is now lying on the banks of the New Canal, near Claiborne Street, is to be sold at public auction today, by the United States authorities, at 12 o'clock, at the Canal Street entrance of the Custom House. The boat in question, which is built of iron and weighs about two tons, was sunk in the Canal about the time of the occupation of the Federal forces, in 1862. It was built as an experiment, and was never fully perfected, and is only valuable now for the machinery and iron which is in and about it.

Later that same day in a later edition, the newspaper printed a short excerpt which read: "The torpedo boat, of which we made mention this morning, was sold at public auction today, at noon, for forty-three dollars. It cost, originally, twenty-six hundred."[15]

In 1878, while digging a canal along the Lake Pontchartrain shoreline just outside New Orleans, workers on the dredge boat *Valentine* discovered a rusting object that appeared to be an old boiler. The object was dragged upon the shore to get it out of the way, and there it remained.

On a balmy summer day seventeen years later, in 1895, Alfred Wellborn and three young friends were walking along the marshy edge of Lake Pontchartrain. They stumbled upon an iron object partially sunk in the mud and hidden by tangled underbrush. The object appeared to be an iron boat and Wellborn suspected it might be one of the Confederate submarines built during the war which he had heard about. He brought the news to a group of men building a wharf nearby, but there was little interest. Returning several months later, Wellborn was surprised to find that the boat had been recovered and was now on display at Spanish Fort.

In 1909 the boat was moved to Camp Nicholls which had become the Louisiana State Home for Confederate veterans. There the submarine remained on display for many years. In 1926, writer and historian William Morrison, Jr., closely examined the relic at the soldier's home and reported his findings:

"She is an even 20 feet in length over all, her greatest inside width is but 3 feet 2 inches, and her maximum depth is 6 feet. In plan view her curves are very pleasing. In mid-ship cross-section, she suggests a racing yacht model. She is fabricated of 1/4-inch iron sheets, fastened with 5/8-inch countersunk rivets. The deck plates are curved to conic sections."

"The propeller—the blades are now broken off—was turned by cranks operated by two men, sitting on little iron brackets fastened, opposite, on each side of the vessel, immediately under the hatchway. There were rudders on either end, connected for single control. The bow rudder is gone, the stock being snapped off just below the rudderpost. The stern rudder is buried in the concrete base, but a photograph taken before the emplacement shows it to be an equipoise-rudder. The diving was accomplished by two side vanes, or fins, 35 inches long by 16 inches wide, placed about on the level of the propeller and over the forward rudder. They both worked on the same shaft, rotated by a lever arm, which directly pointed the angle of the dive. The port vane has been twisted off."

"The sole entrance to the vessel is through the 18-inch hatchway amidships. The edge of the opening is reinforced with an iron collar, 3/8-inch thick and 2 1/2 inches wide. The cover is gone, but the indications are that it was simply a lid hinged aft and closing on a gasket fastened directly to the curved roof or deck; for the rivet holes surrounding the hatch are only 1/8-inch in diameter. It does not seem probable that the cover stood high enough, as in the *Hunley,* to serve as a conning tower with eyeports. In fact, little provision seems to have been made for light or observation. In the roof, forward of the hatch, there are two groups of eight 3/4-inch holes, each, arranged in circles one foot in diameter. These holes may have been glassed, serving as small light-ports. Surmounting the center of the more forward set of holes is a cuff, five inches in height and in diameter, which seems to have been a stuffing box through which an air shaft passed.... There is in the prow or nose of the vessel a 2-inch circular opening, which, I am inclined to believe, was used for forward observation rather than as a socket for a torpedo spar."[16]

On April 24, 1957, the submarine was sent to its final location. Acquired by the Louisiana State Museum, the vessel was moved to the arcade of the Presbytere, just outside Jackson Square in New Orleans. Now protected by the museum, it is finally safe from the elements. One researcher, Francis Chandler Furman, has suggested that this boat may, in fact, be one of the submersibles reportedly constructed at the Tredegar Iron Works in Richmond. If this is the case, its small size may indicate that it was constructed as a builder's scale working prototype which may have been shipped via rail to New Orleans at the request of Edward M. Ives, Tredegar's New Orleans agent. There it would have been used to assist as a pattern for larger boats which were intended to be built by the Confederate Navy.[17]

For many years this submarine has been misidentified as the *Pioneer*. Recent research has proven, however, that Hunley, McClintock, and Watson did, indeed, sink their invention in the New Basin Canal, and that it was later dredged up and sold at public auction. Most likely the boat was broken up and the iron sold as scrap. Other than the theory proposed by Furman, the origins of the second submarine found are a mystery to this day. One detail, however, is known for sure. The boat at the Louisiana State Museum is definitely not the *Pioneer*.[18]

   With New Orleans in enemy hands, and Hunley, McClintock, and Watson safely in Mobile, the intriguing story of the yet to be CSS *H. L. Hunley* shifts now to that historic city in Alabama.

Major General Mansfield Lovell, Confederate military commander at New Orleans
Library of Congress

John K. Scott squeezes through the narrow hatch of the _Pioneer_ at a dock in New Orleans.
Drawing by Greg Cottrell, courtesy of Mark K. Ragan

A blank letter of Marque and Reprisal of the type issued by the Confederate government. The *Pioneer*, under the command of John K. Scott, was granted such a commission.

National Archives

14

Three views of the small submarine that for years had been misidentified as the *Pioneer*. The boat is now part of the Louisiana State Museum in New Orleans. The designer and builder of this submarine are still unknown.

William M. Robinson, *Confederate Privateers*

Recently discovered diagram of the CSS *Pioneer* drawn by Engineer William Shock of the USS *Pensacola* after the fall of New Orleans.

National Archives, courtesy of Mark K. Ragan

James R. McClintock

Chapter Two
The American Diver

Arriving in Mobile shortly after the loss of New Orleans, Hunley, Watson, and McClintock sought out the military commander of the district, Major General Dabney H. Maury. The general was the nephew of famous oceanographer and underwater explosive expert, Matthew Fountain Maury, and was eager to employ any method he could find to shore up the defenses of the city and the bay. Fascinated by the drawings and diagrams unrolled by the three, Maury promised his full support in their endeavor to construct another submarine boat.

At this time in the life of the new Confederate nation, Mobile was humming with wartime activity. Being a major railroad hub, army regiments were consistently passing through on their way to the eastern and western fronts. Machine shops and foundries abounded, turning the atmosphere a dirty gray with the smoke from their chimneys. Mechanics, engineers, and machinists were detached from army units and placed on temporary duty in these facilities in order to aid the production of war material.

One of those soldiers placed on detached duty in Mobile was a young sandy-bearded British-born mechanical engineer by the name of William Alexander. A lieutenant in the 21st Alabama Infantry Regiment, Alexander had enlisted in Company B, commanded by Captain Charles Gage, at the beginning of hostilities. After sustaining heavy casualties at the Battle of Shiloh, the 21st Alabama was sent to Mobile where Alexander was ordered to the machine shop owned by Thomas Park and Thomas B. Lyons. The facility was conveniently located near the harbor on Water Street.[1]

Alexander and the other workers had been engaged in rifling the barrels of hundreds of outdated Mississippi Rifles when Hunley, Watson, and McClintock walked through the front door. The plans and diagrams were spread before the supervisor of the shop and the request made to begin construction. Although the idea of building an underwater craft must have seemed inconceivable to many of the machinists, the backing of General Maury conveyed a sense of reality to the request. Alexander was told to suspend all of his work on the Mississippi Rifles and devote the shop's entire effort toward building the boat.

The selection of the Park & Lyons company was a wise choice. Its excellent facilities included two large cranes and a foundry that could produce almost any part imaginable. It was a commonly accepted fact that the Park & Lyons facility was one of the best machine shops in the city of Mobile. With such admirable capabilities, it was not long before the outline of this next submarine began to take shape on the shop floor. Records are frustratingly scanty concerning this boat, but it is known that Horace Hunley provided the entire source of funds for materials and construction. Confusion still reigns, however, over the exact name of the boat. Late in the war a Confederate deserter by the name of Belton who had worked at Park & Lyons called her the *American Diver*. On the other hand, Belton, who deserted from the Confederate Navy in Charleston, may have been referring to the *Hunley*. Likewise, some historians have referred to this second boat as the *Pioneer II*. It is possible that no "official" name was ever given to this second craft, but for the sake of clarity this author will refer to her as the *American Diver*.[2]

From what is known about the *American Diver*, it appears that several months were lost in attempting to adopt a unique form of propulsion. In his letter to Commander Maury, McClintock wrote that:

"To obtain room for the machinery and persons, she was built 36 feet long, 3 feet wide and 4 feet high, 12 feet at each end was built tapering or modeled to make her easy to pass through the water. There was much time and money lost in efforts to build an electro-magnetic engine to propel the boat....I afterwards fitted cranks to turn the propeller by hand, working four men at a time."[3]

A most valuable source of information on McClintock's submersible boat building activities are several documents and sketches recently uncovered at the Public Record Office (PRO) in London. In late October of 1872, according to these records, McClintock traveled from Mobile to Halifax, Nova Scotia to attend a secret meeting with a group of Royal Navy officers aboard the HMS *Royal Alfred*. The purpose of the trip was to discuss his work in submarine warfare, and to propose that he build a submersible torpedo vessel for the Royal Navy. Captain F. Nicholson, RN, and Chief Engineer J. H. Ellis, RN, of the *Royal Alfred* were instructed to meet with him, gather as much information as possible, and report their findings and recommendations in writing to the admiralty. The meeting was secretive, most likely to protect McClintock, for divulging such sensitive technical information to a foreign power could have been construed as treasonous, especially if he had been required to swear an oath of allegiance at the end of the war. In their ensuing report, Nicholson and Ellis recorded that they were: "thoroughly impressed with the intelligence of Mr. McClintock, and with his knowledge of all points chemical and mechanical connected with torpedoes and submarine vessels....He is, I believe, entirely self-taught, and was much employed by the Confederates on torpedo work, on which he has much practical information which he seems ready to communicate. He hates his countrymen, Americans, and hopes to some day be a British subject."

At this meeting, McClintock provided additional detail concerning the *American Diver*:

"In 1863 I built the second boat, also of iron ¼ inch thick, and in order to obtain more room as well as to correct the faults of the first boat, she was built with square sides. Dimensions were 36 feet long, 4 feet high, and 3 feet across top & bottom, with ends tapered like a wedge for a model, with a 30 inch propeller in the end. I spent much time and money in efforts to work an Electro Magnetic Engine, but without success. I afterwards fitted her up with cranks, to be turned by four men. But her speed was not sufficient to make her of service against blockaders, they being six miles at sea."[4]

The origin of the electromagnetic engine is obscure, and as a result it has been the subject of much speculation. McClintock may have been influenced by several descriptions of electromagnetic engines which appeared in the British technical publication *The Engineer*. This seems plausible in light of the fact that at the meeting in Halifax, he referenced this same publication when proposing an ammoniacally-powered submarine to the Royal Navy. Power for this engine was to be provided by large batteries mounted in series so as to produce the maximum amount of voltage. The "magnetic engine," as it was called, had been invented in 1829 by Joseph Henry, a scientist who was now applying his innovative mind to helping the North. This motor was a reverse magnet, which instead of converting mechanical energy into electricity, did the opposite. It was the forerunner of the electric motor that we know today. McClintock brought in an expert from New Orleans to mount the engine, but the endeavor proved unsuccessful. Although this means of propulsion was a failure, the very idea of attempting to build and employ such a device illustrates how far ahead of their time the builders really were.[5]

With the idea of an electromagnetic engine discarded, the designers next turned their attention to the steam engine. While it was obvious that any steam engine would quickly deplete the available oxygen in a submerged boat, evidence seems to indicate that McClintock had another concept in mind. If a specially built engine was run on the surface, building up a high pressure of steam, the boat then might continue submerged on the remaining pressure after the engine was shut down. This concept, too, proved to be more than could be constructed at the time. Ironically, this same idea proved very successful later in an experimental European submarine.[6]

With the failure of the electric motor and the steam engine, McClintock removed the machinery and installed a propeller shaft designed to be turned by four men. By mid-January 1863, the *American Diver* was ready for her initial trials. The first test revealed that the boat was awkward to handle and extremely difficult to propel manually. McClintock wrote that "...the air being so close and the work so hard, we were unable to get a speed sufficient to make the boat of service against vessels blockading this port."[7]

Late in 1862, Admiral Franklin Buchanan, former commander of the ironclad CSS *Virginia* in the historic first day's battle in Hampton Roads, Virginia, was dispatched to Mobile to take charge of the naval defenses of the city. Buchanan, a student of the "old school" of naval tactics, felt that underwater assaults, whether in the form of mines or submarines, were against the principles of civilized warfare. As a consequence, his letter to Secretary of the Navy, Stephen R. Mallory, on February 14, 1863, was highly critical of McClintock's invention. Nevertheless, Buchanan's letter to the secretary sheds much light on the experiments with the *American Diver* and its subsequent loss:

"Sir: I have the honor to acknowledge the receipt of your letter of the 27th relating to Mr. McClintock's submarine boat. Mr. McClintock has received from this state, from General Slaughter commanding her, and from myself all the assistance and facilities he requested to complete his boat, and within the last week or ten days we succeeded in getting a man from New Orleans who was to have made the 'magnetic engine' by which it was to have been propelled. I have witnessed the operations of the boat in the water when propelled by hand, the steam engine being a failure and had to be removed."

"On that occasion its speed was not more than two miles per hour. Since then other trials have been made all proving failures. The last trial was made about a week since when the boat was lost off this harbor and was sunk, the men came very near being lost. I never entertained but one opinion as to the result of this boat, that it should prove a failure, and such has been the case. The original intention of going under a vessel and attaching a torpedo to her was abandoned, the torpedo or explosive machine was to have been towed by a rope from the boat and when under the vessel was to have been exploded. I considered the whole affair as impracticable from the commencement."[8]

From the above letter it seems clear that the *American Diver* did not live up to the expectations of McClintock, Watson, and Hunley. Further clarification on the loss of the boat is provided by a small excerpt in a 1902 article written by William Alexander which appeared in the *Southern Historical Society Papers*: "It (the submarine) was towed off Ft. Morgan, intended to man it there and attack the blockading fleet outside, but the weather was rough, and with a heavy sea the boat became unmanageable and finally sank, but no lives were lost."[9]

The trio of designers and builders must have been devastated by the loss, but they were determined to continue their tests. At first there was some thought of salvaging the *American Diver*. Shortly after the sinking, Buchanan received a short inquiry concerning the submarine from the naval Secretary. It appears that Watson had written to Mallory informing him of the loss and requesting some form of government assistance in raising the vessel. Mallory's inquiry to Buchanan seemed to question whether such an endeavor was justified. In response, Buchanan sent him the following communication:

"Hon: S. R. Mallory, Secretary of the Navy, Richmond, Va.

Sir. I have the honor to acknowledge the receipt of your letter of the 23rd with enclosed communication from Baxter Watson relating to his submarine boat. On the 14th I addressed you on that subject. Mr. McClintock spoken of by me was one of the partners associated with Mr. Watson. The boat can not be of any possible use in Mobile Bay in consequence of its shallow water. I don't think it could be made effective against the enemy off the harbor as the blockading vessels are anchored in water too shallow to permit the boat to pass under."[10]

It was now apparent that the builders had no hope of salvaging the *American Diver*. The war continued on and while discouraged, the builders were convinced that their design was sound and so began work on a third boat. Out in Mobile Bay, not far from the frowning ramparts of Fort Morgan, the rusting remains of the *American Diver* remain to this day. It is unfortunate that she never had the opportunity to prove her merit against the numerous blockading ships of the enemy fleet, but lessons learned in her brief existence would soon be incorporated into the third and final boat now taking shape on the floor of the Park & Lyons machine shop.

Horace Lawson Hunley

Naval Historical Center

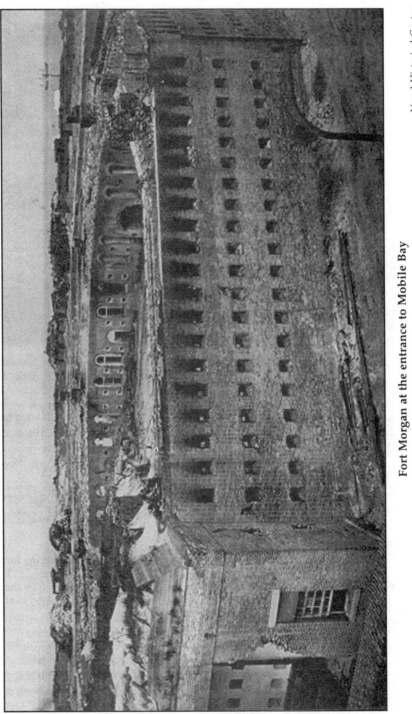

Fort Morgan at the entrance to Mobile Bay

Naval Historical Center

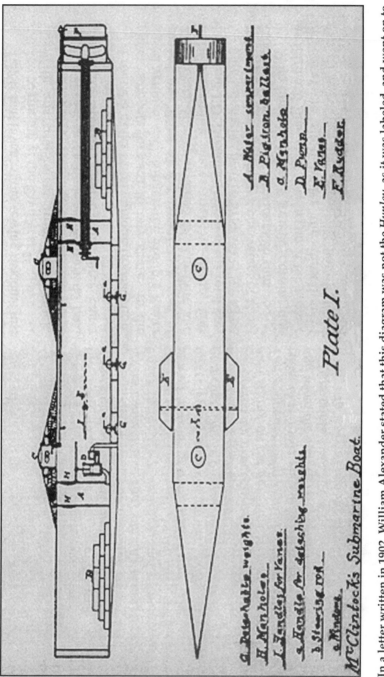

Plate I.

McClintock's Submarine Boat.

a. Detachable weights.
H. Manholes.
I. Handles for Vanes.
s. Lever for detaching weights.
b. Steering rod.
a. Windows.

A. Water compartment.
B. Pig iron ballast.
a. Manhole.
D. Pump.
E. Vanes.
F. Rudder.

In a letter written in 1902, William Alexander stated that this diagram was not the *Hunley*, as it was labeled, and went on to write: "After the capture of New Orleans, McClintock went to Mobile where he built the submarine in plate 1."

U.S. Naval Institute, courtesy of Mark K. Ragan

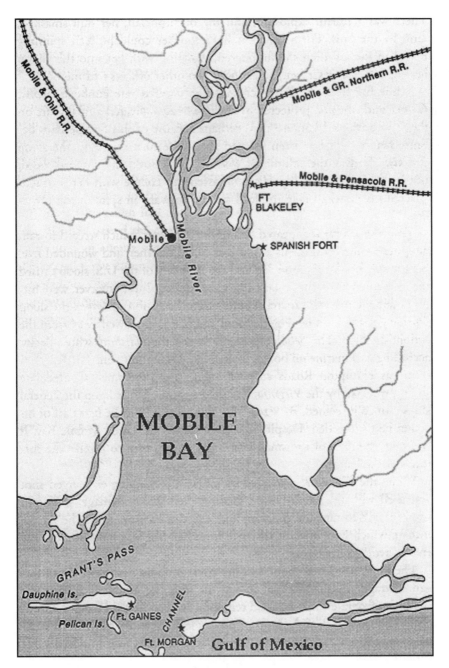

Map of Mobile Bay

Major General Dabney H. Maury, military commander of the District of Mobile

Library of Congress

The Park and Lyons machine shop at the corner of Water and State Streets in Mobile, Alabama. Both the *American Diver* and the *Hunley* were constructed here. This photo was taken in 1960, but, unfortunately, the building has since been torn down.

Naval Historical Center

Chapter Three
The *Hunley* at Mobile

It is not known how much Horace Hunley invested in the *American Diver*, but it is assumed to have been a considerable amount. To lose the boat before she had an opportunity to engage the enemy was particularly devastating. The trio were determined, however, to build another and better underseas craft, but how was it to be financed? Fortunately, at about this time, an organization of engineers sympathetic to the Confederate cause had been formed in Mobile with Hunley, McClintock, and Watson being among the members. This group was charged with "the special service of destroying the enemy's property by torpedoes and similar inventions."[1] Under regulations established by the Confederate government, the organization would be entitled to fifty percent of the value of any enemy vessel destroyed by means of their contrivance. Founder of the group was a self-styled mechanical engineer by the name of E. C. Singer, who currently produced the most reliable underwater torpedo for the Confederacy. Prior to the war, Singer's uncle had invented the sewing machine which bore his name.[2]

The Singer Submarine Corps, undoubtedly influenced by the urging of Hunley, McClintock, and Watson, decided to invest in the construction of the next underwater boat. Five men of this organization purchased shares in what was to become the *H. L. Hunley*. Singer invested one-third of the cost of the vessel which amounted to $5,000, while Hunley, his resources not quite depleted by the *American Diver*, invested another third. The remaining shares were divided among R. W. Dunn, who purchased a $2,000 share, and B. Gus Whitney and J. D. Breaman who together bought a $3,000 interest. This brought the total cost of the proposed submarine boat to $15,000. In today's value of gold, this was equivalent to approximately $300,000.

This third boat was constructed during the spring of 1863, in the same Park & Lyons shop where the *American Diver* had taken shape. The builders "took more pains with her model and machinery," McClintock recorded, designing the submarine from the beginning to be powered by eight men turning a central crank connected to a propeller. A ninth crew member would act as captain and helmsman. Sometime during this period the boat was christened *H. L. Hunley* in honor of her principal supporter.

With financial backing secured, and avoiding the mistakes made in the *American Diver*, mechanics at the Park & Lyons shop made good progress in fitting the *Hunley* together. Writing for the *Southern Historical Society Papers* in 1902, Lieutenant Alexander gave a detailed description of her:

"We decided to build another boat, and for this purpose took a cylinder boiler which we had on hand, 48 inches in diameter and 25 feet long (all dimensions are from memory). We cut this boiler in two, longitudinally, and inserted two 12-inch boiler iron strips in her sides; lengthened her by one tapering course fore and aft, to which were attached bow and stem castings, making the boat about 40 feet long, 4 feet wide and 5 feet deep. A longitudinal strip 12 inches wide was riveted the full length on top. At each end a bulkhead was riveted across to form water-ballast tanks (unfortunately these were left open on top); they were used in raising and sinking the boat. In addition to these water tanks the boat was ballasted by flat castings, made to fit the outside bottom of the shell and fastened thereto by 'Tee' headed bolts passing through stuffing boxes inside the boat, the inside end of the bolt squared to fit a wrench, that the bolts might be turned and the ballast dropped, should the necessity arise."

"In connection with each of the water tanks, there was a sea-cock open to the sea to supply the tank for sinking; also a force pump to eject the water from the tanks into the sea for raising the boat to the surface. There was also a bilge connection to the pump. A mercury gauge, open to the sea, was attached to the shell near the forward tank, to indicate the depth of the boat below the surface. A one and a quarter inch shaft passed through stuffing boxes on each side of the boat, just forward of the end of the propeller shaft. On each side of this shaft, outside of the boat, castings, or lateral fins, five feet long and eight inches wide, were secured. This shaft was operated by a lever amidships, and by raising or lowering the ends of these fins, operated as the fins of a fish, changing the depth of the boat below the surface at will, without disturbing the water level in the ballast tanks."

"The rudder was operated by a wheel, and levers connected to rods passing through stuffing boxes in the stern castings, and operated by the captain or pilot forward. An adjusted compass was placed in front of the forward tank. The boat was operated by manual power, with an ordinary propeller. On the propelling shaft there were formed eight cranks at different angles; the shaft was supported by brackets on the starboard side, the men sitting on the port side turning on the cranks. The propeller shaft and cranks took up so much room that it was very difficult to pass fore and aft, and when the men were in their places this was next to impossible."

"In operation, one half of the crew had to pass through the fore hatch; the other through the after hatchway. The propeller revolved in a wrought iron ring or band, to guard against a line being thrown in to foul it. There were two hatchways one fore and one aft—16 inches by 12, with a combing 8 inches high. These hatches had hinged covers with rubber gaskets, and were bolted from the inside. In the sides and ends of these combings glasses were inserted to sight from. There was an opening made in the top of the boat for an air box, a casting with a close top 12 by 18 by 4 inches, made to carry a hollow shaft. This shaft passed through stuffing boxes. On each end was an elbow with a 4 foot length of 1½-inch pipe, and keyed to the hollow shaft; on the inside was a lever with a stopcock to admit air."[3]

During this period of time, another young lieutenant from the 21st Alabama was detailed to the enterprise. He was George E. Dixon and forever would be linked with the history and legacy of the *H. L. Hunley.* Dixon was a native of Kentucky and had entered Confederate service in the spring of 1861. At the time of his enlistment in the army, he was serving as an engineer officer on board a Mississippi River boat. Wounded at Shiloh with a severe leg injury, he was sent to Mobile to recuperate which may also explain why he was relieved from active field duty and ordered to the Park & Lyons shop.[4]

During construction, Horace Hunley was continually being called away from Mobile to provide other services for the Confederacy. On May 4, 1863, he was in central Mississippi on military business. Hunley, who apparently was engaged in various enterprises for the government, acted as a secret agent assisting in the running of arms and ammunition through the blockade. An additional burden was placed upon him by the pressing need to dispose of his large holdings in cotton, sugar, and tobacco. Worried over the progress of the submarine at the shop in Mobile, he consistently besieged McClintock with letters begging for details and imploring him to hasten the construction. If the

Hunley were successful, others could be built and transported to the many blockaded ports. With the anticipated success of the boat, Hunley believed the blockade could be broken and independence won.[5]

In mid-July 1863, shortly after the devastating news of the defeat at Gettysburg and the loss of Vicksburg had reached Mobile, the *H. L. Hunley* slid down wooden ramps into the harbor near the Theater Street dock. Reports indicate that a small crowd had gathered to watch the launching, but it is doubtful that any appreciated the historic significance of this event. None could possibly have imagined how radically this futuristic new invention would change the nature of naval warfare.

It was immediately apparent that this submarine was a marked improvement over the *Pioneer* and the *American Diver*. Applying the lessons learned with the previous two boats, the tests revealed that the *Hunley* handled well, and was faster and more maneuverable than its predecessors. To keep the boat from tilting while under way, an assigned spot was given to each of the eight men at the propeller crank where they were to remain without moving.

All seams and crevices were tightly sealed on the interior, and wrought iron ladders led up to each hatch. The captain stood so that when the boat was partially submerged, he could sight through the glass of the combings of the forward hatch. At his hands were the diving lever which controlled the vanes on the exterior, a sea cock used to flood the forward ballast tank, a hand pump to pump out the water, a mercury depth gauge (manometer), a magnetic compass, and a small ship's wheel connected to the rudder. A petty officer occupied the rear hatch position with a sea cock and hand pump to control the aft ballast tank. Interior light was provided by a single candle, and when the flame went out in 20 to 25 minutes, it was an indication that there was a minimum supply of oxygen and it was time to surface for air. When launched in the spring of 1863, the *Hunley* measured forty feet long and was the best underwater boat that had been completed to date. Considering all the handicaps and shortages under which the Confederacy was struggling, it is simply amazing that such a unique and sophisticated craft was designed and built at all.[6]

McClintock later described this boat: "In the Spring of 1864, I built the 3rd boat, having abandoned the artificial motive power as not attainable in our situations. I modeled her, and built expressly for hand power. This boat was of an elliptic shape, with modeled ends, and looked similar to surf, or whale boats, placed one on top of the other. She was built of iron 3/8 inch thick, 40 feet long top & bottom, 42 inches wide in the middle, & 48 inches high, fitted with cranks geared to her propeller and turned by eight persons inside of her. And although she was a beautiful model boat, and worked to perfection just like her predecessors, the power was too uncertain to admit of her venturing far from shore."[7]

Serious testing now began at Mobile. Unfortunately, surviving records do not reveal who captained the boat during these early trials, but it most likely was Dixon or McClintock. Crew members were probably some of the mechanics from the machine shop. The *Hunley* proved easy to manage in the calm waters of the Mobile River. The designers, however, remembering the fate of the *American Diver*, were not yet ready to commit the boat to the choppy waters of Mobile Bay.

At the conclusion of the initial trials, McClintock and Watson were so satisfied that they arranged a demonstration for Admiral Franklin Buchanan, Mobile's naval commander. Buchanan, the Confederacy's only admiral (Raphael Semmes would later, after the loss of the CSS *Alabama*, be promoted to rear admiral) was born near Baltimore, Maryland in 1800, and had been the first commandant of the U.S. Naval Academy when the school opened in 1845. Now sixty-three, the crusty admiral was of the "old school" and viewed such inventions as underwater torpedoes (or mines) and submarine boats as "infernal machines" which were inhuman in their form of attack on the enemy. Nevertheless, the Confederacy was struggling for its very existence and any invention that might turn the tide was worth considering. Buchanan agreed to come to the demonstration.

Early on the morning of July 31, 1863, an old flat boat, used for hauling coal, was towed to the middle of the Mobile River and anchored. Several high-ranking military officers, including Buchanan, had gathered on the shore to witness the demonstration. Farther upstream, the crew of the *Hunley* was squeezing through the open hatches. When all were aboard, the skipper ordered the hatches secured, and he and the second officer at the aft hatch opened the sea-valves to emit water into the ballast tanks. Slowly, as the dignitaries watched from shore, the submarine began to sink lower and lower until only her two combings were visible. When the water began to appear at the bottom of the small glass viewing-port in the forward hatch tower, the commander ordered the valves closed, lit the candle, and the crew to begin turning the propeller crank. Swinging the wheel to position the rudder, the *Hunley* headed for her intended victim.

Prior to this test, a Confederate torpedo had been attached to the boat. Writing after the war, Alexander gives us a good picture of just how this early torpedo was supposed to work:

"The torpedo was a copper cylinder holding a charge of ninety pounds of explosive, with percussion and friction primer mechanism, set off by flaring triggers. It was originally intended to float the torpedo on the surface of the water, the boat to dive under the vessel to be attacked, towing the torpedo with a line 200 feet after her, one of the triggers to touch the vessel and explode the torpedo, and in the experiments made in the smooth water of Mobile River on some old flatboats these plans operated successfully, but in rough water the torpedo was continually coming too near the submarine boat."[8]

With the boat under way, the captain, peering through the tiny glass view-port, steered for the flat boat while carefully taking note of his magnetic compass heading. Trailing behind at a respectable distance, and hardly perceptible to the onlookers on shore, came the deadly torpedo. The word had spread and by now there was a sizable crowd gathered along the river. As the *Hunley* neared the flat boat, the captain gently depressed the diving handle and the boat, to a collective gasp from the onlookers, disappeared beneath the surface.

Carefully watching the mercury depth gauge in the light of the flickering candle, the skipper held the diving handle in the down position until twenty feet registered on the glass, at which point he brought the lever back to neutral. A pocket watch was produced, and the captain, making minor adjustments of the wheel based on the gently swinging compass, counted the seconds while the crew continued the furious revolving of the propeller crank. Suddenly a muffled explosion could be heard followed by a tremendous concussion as the compressed water slammed into the *Hunley*. The boat rolled violently from side to side as the skipper raised the diving lever with one hand and began pumping the ballast tank with the other. The second officer at the rear hatch began pumping the aft tank, and within seconds the *Hunley* broke the surface. The hatches were thrown open and the cheers of those gathered on shore could be distinctly heard. Looking back, only a layer of bubbles, smoke, and debris marked where the coal barge had once been. The *Hunley* had unquestionably proven herself as a viable weapon against the ever-tightening Federal blockade.[9]

Even Admiral Buchanan was convinced. The following day, he penned a letter to his good friend John Tucker, commander of the naval defenses at Charleston, South Carolina:

"Naval Commandant's Office, Mobile, Ala. August 1st, 1863.
Sir. I yesterday witnessed the destruction of a lighter, or coal flat, in the Mobile River by a torpedo which was placed under it by a submarine iron boat, the invention of Messrs. Whitney and McClintock. Messrs. Watson and Whitney visit Charleston for the purpose of consulting General Beauregard and yourself to ascertain whether you will try it, they will explain all its advantages, and if it can operate in smooth water where the current is not strong as was the case yesterday. I can recommend it to your favorable consideration. It can be propelled about four knots per hour, to judge from the experiment of yesterday. I am fully satisfied it can be used successfully in blowing-up one or more of the enemy's ironclads in your harbor. Do me the favor to show this to General Beauregard with my regards.
Very Respectfully Franklin Buchanan, Admiral CSN."[10]

Those familiar with the area, and now that would have included, Hunley, McClintock, and Watson, were cognizant of the fact that while the *Hunley* might be successful in the placid waters of the Mobile River, she could easily suffer the same fate as the *American Diver* if subjected to the rolling swells and violent waves of the Gulf of Mexico. The suggestion, therefore, of transferring the submarine to the more tranquil waters of Charleston harbor was welcomed with genuine enthusiasm by the designers in Mobile. Perhaps, at last, their invention would have the opportunity to display its attacking capabilities against an enemy warship.

To arrange for the transfer, Baxter Watson and Gus Whitney traveled to Charleston, seeking a meeting with the area's military commander, General Pierre Gustave Toutant Beauregard. The Creole general was eager to do anything that would improve the defenses of Charleston and welcomed the two into his headquarters. Beauregard had been shown the letter from Buchanan and watched with interest as the two men from Mobile unrolled their strange diagrams and explained the operations of the submarine boat. With Federal pressure mounting on the besieged city, the commanding general wasted little time in approving the transfer of the *Hunley* to Charleston. On August 7, 1863, a terse telegram crackled over the wires between Charleston and Mobile: "Quartermasters and Railroad Agents on lines from Charleston, S. C., to Mobile Alabama: Please expedite transportation of Whitney's submarine boat from Mobile here. It is much needed."[11]

Upon receipt of the telegram in Mobile, the *Hunley* was pulled from the water in August of 1863, and hauled to the Mobile and Great Northern Railroad yard at Tenas Landing. Here the forty-foot boat was hoisted aboard two flatcars for the trip to Charleston.

In a letter sent to his fiancée, Lieutenant George W. Gift, an officer on the CSS *Gaines*, described how he had "been employed during the past day or two in hoisting out of the water and sending away toward Charleston, a very curious machine for destroying vessels...."

"In the first place imagine a high pressure steam boiler, not quite round, say 4 feet in diameter in one way and 3½ feet the other—draw each end of the boiler down to a sharp wedge shaped point. The 4 feet is the depth of the hold and the 3½ feet the breadth of beam. On the bottom of the boat is riveted an iron keel weighing 4,000 lb. which throws the center of gravity on one side and makes her swim steadily that side down. On top and opposite the keel is placed two man hole plates or hatches with heavy glass tops. These plates are water tight when covered over. They are just large enough for a man to go in and out. At one end is fitted a very neat little propeller 3½ feet in diameter worked by men sitting in the boat and turning the shaft by hand cranks being fitted on it for that purpose. She also has a rudder and steering apparatus."

"Embarked and under ordinary circumstances with men, ballast, etc., she floats about half way out of the water and resembles a whale. But when it is necessary to go under the water there are apartments into which the water is allowed to flow, which causes the boat to sink to any required depth, the same being accurately indicated by a column of mercury. Air is supplied by means of pipes that turn up until they get below a depth of 10 feet, when they must depend upon the supply carried down which is sufficient for 3 hours! During which time she could have been propelled 15 miles!"

"Behind the boat at a distance of 100 to 150 feet is towed a plank and under that plank is attached a torpedo with say 100 lb. of powder. The steersman has a string by which he can explode the torpedo by giving it a jerk. I saw them explode a vessel as an experiment. They approached within about fifty yards of her keeping the man holes just above water. At that distance she, the submarine, sank down and in a few minutes made her appearance on the other side of the vessel. He pulled the string and smashed her side to atoms...."[12]

With Gift's labors completed, the *Hunley,* firmly chocked in place and probably shrouded by canvas, was about to begin her long journey. McClintock and Whitney were designated to accompany the boat to Charleston along with a few hand-picked engineers and mechanics from the Park & Lyons shop. The trip would take the band of adventurers and their invention from Mobile to Pollard, Alabama where the road joined the Alabama and Florida rail line. From there the route would take them through Selma, Alabama, to Atlanta, Georgia, then to Augusta, Georgia, and finally on to Charleston.

On the morning of August 10, the journey began. In a cloud of steam and black smoke, the train and its precious cargo pulled out of the Tenas yard. For the group of men riding in the passenger car behind the shrouded *Hunley,* it was a time of mixed emotions as they said good-bye to Mobile and looked forward with anxious anticipation to the besieged city of Charleston.[13]

An autographed likeness of James R. McClintock
Naval Historical Center

Stephen R. Mallory, secretary
of the Confederate States
Navy
        Naval Historical Center

Admiral Franklin Buchanan,
Confederate naval commander
at Mobile, Alabama
        Naval Historical Center

William Alexander as he appeared in the spring of 1902
Museum of the City of Mobile, courtesy of Mark K. Ragan

38

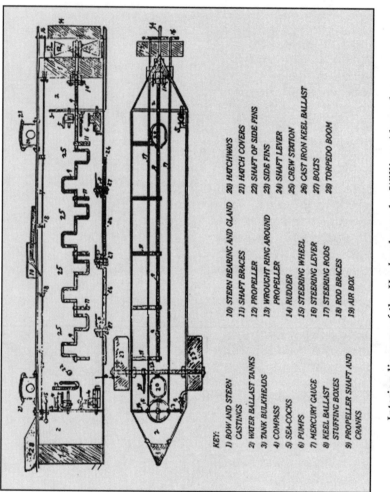

Interior diagram of the *Hunley* drawn by William Alexander.

Official Records Navy

KEY:

1) BOW AND STERN CASTINGS
2) WATER BALLAST TANKS
3) TANK BULKHEADS
4) COMPASS
5) SEA-COCKS
6) PUMPS
7) MERCURY GAUGE
8) KEEL BALLAST STUFFING BOXES
9) PROPELLER SHAFT AND CRANKS

10) STERN BEARING AND GLAND
11) SHAFT BRACES
12) PROPELLER
13) WROUGHT RING AROUND PROPELLER
14) RUDDER
15) STEERING WHEEL
16) STEERING LEVER
17) STEERING RODS
18) ROD BRACES
19) AIR BOX

20) HATCHWAYS
21) HATCH COVERS
22) SHAFT OF SIDE FINS
23) SIDE FINS
24) SHAFT LEVER
25) CREW STATION
26) CAST IRON KEEL BALLAST
27) BOLTS
28) TORPEDO BOOM

Chapter Four

Disaster at Charleston

Unlike Mobile, which had yet to experience the war firsthand, Charleston was continually in the thick of the fighting. Despised by the Federals, the beautiful but defiant city was nestled between the Ashley and Cooper Rivers, and was looked upon by most Northerners as the heart of the "rebellion." Incensed at not being able to reduce this "Hotbed of Secession," the Union government continued to send additional men, munitions, and warships to the area in an effort to pound the city into submission.

By August of 1863, Charleston's primary defensive position consisted of Fort Sumter, which was located at the outer entrance to the harbor. Fort Sumter, where the "first" shots of the war had been exchanged over two years before, was garrisoned by approximately 350 men with 79 cannons of various caliber. Fort Moultrie, situated at the southern end of Sullivan's Island and manned by 300 troops with 38 guns, guarded the northern channel between it and Fort Sumter. Stretching between Sumter and Moultrie was a strong line of underwater torpedoes which had been anchored to keep the enemy ironclads at bay. Guarding the southern entrance of the harbor, was Battery Wagner at the tip of Morris Island. Battery Wagner was currently under a vicious and direct land attack from the Federal infantry which had recently occupied the southern end of the island.[1]

On the morning of August 12, 1863, the train hauling the small submarine and her weary crew from Mobile steamed slowly into the bustling Charleston railroad station. With Union pressure mounting daily, military leaders in the desperate city had waited eagerly for the arrival of the little diving machine that they all hoped would put an end to the terrible siege.

An indication of just how anxious military headquarters was concerning the safe arrival of the *Hunley* is revealed in a telegram sent to General Dabney Maury in Mobile: "August 11, 1863, General Maury, has the submarine boat been sent from Mobile (stop) if so when did it leave for Charleston (stop) Signed G. T. Beauregard general commanding."[2]

As the train bearing the *Hunley* squealed to a stop, McClintock and his exhausted crew stepped from their railroad car into a scene far different from that in Mobile. Charleston was a city at war. Most impressive was the dull rumble of heavy guns which could be heard over the noise of the busy train station. Military wagons and carts clattered over the dusty streets. Army units and gangs of African-Americans, who were used to repair the damaged fortifications, hurried by as they rushed to their assigned positions in the siege lines. Wide-eyed children clung to their mother's side, and disabled and wounded soldiers were a common sight. This was war, and now McClintock and his men were in the middle of it.

General Beauregard ordered the engineering department to unload the *Hunley* and transfer it to a nearby slip as soon as possible. Even before the submarine had been lifted from the flatcars, word had spread throughout the city of its safe arrival. Soon a small crowd had gathered to watch as men and mules strained at the heavy ropes that were used to lift the *Hunley* from its cradle. Swung free of the rail cars, the boat was rolled through the streets to the accompaniment of cheering crowds waving Confederate flags. Many truly believed that this diminutive machine represented their best hope at ending the nightmare that had engulfed the city.

On the same day as the sub's arrival in Charleston, Beauregard, eager to get the boat into service, issued the following orders: "August 12th 1863. Major Hutson Chief Quartermaster, Department of S. C., Ga., & Fla. You will furnish Mr. B. A. Whitney on his requisition with such articles as he may need for placing his submarine vessel in condition for service. His requisitions will be approved subsequently at this office."[3]

No records exist indicating just where the *Hunley* first entered the waters of Charleston harbor, but judging from the location of the train station it most probably was the small dock at the end of Calhoun Street on the Cooper River. From there it would have been an easy task to tow the boat to any spot in the harbor. Shortly after the boat's arrival, E. C. Singer also detrained in Charleston. Singer came to the South

Carolina city to apply his innovative genius to the building of underwater torpedoes to be placed as a defense against the Federal ironclads.

Still detained in Mississippi, Horace Hunley was nevertheless very interested in the operations at Charleston. In a letter shortly after Singer's arrival, Hunley wrote to McClintock:

"I have been extremely anxious about your experiments at Charleston. It is not at all on the question of whether you will succeed in blowing up a vessel of the enemy, for I think that more than probable and of itself only a small matter. It is whether your success will be made available in effecting a real solid benefit to the Confederacy and conferring glory on it's originators."

"I am anxious first and above all for a dead silence on your part that the enemy may be lost in uncertainty and mystery, which is more dreadful than any understood evil even of the greatest magnitude. Secondly, while in a panic, if you succeed, the enemy if properly pressed before he can make preparations to resist the consequences of your success might possibly be driven entirely from Morris Island, his works destroyed, and guns spiked even if it be not possible to take and permanently hold the island and prevent it from being retaken. Therefore, as I cannot join you, I would be glad to have you in conversation with General Beauregard if this reaches you before your experiment to ask him (by way of suggestion) if you should be so fortunate as to succeed, and if that success should create a panic and consequent retreat, if a rapid descent by vessels and men could not drive the enemy from the island."

"If he should think that a panic and retreat of the enemies could effect such a result, then make every effort first to get him to prepare silently for such an event, and then by at least one spare torpedo for a second attempt make a heroic attempt to produce this panic. Remind your crew of Manassas and Shiloh and the consequences of faltering in the hour of success, and make one grand effort and you may have cause to rejoice over the fruits of your labor, and that like men in more exalted positions, you did not stop to rejoice over your small gains and let slip a vast success and immortal honor. Read this to Whitney. H. L. Hunley."[4]

These were chaotic days in Charleston. All military authorities were eager for McClintock and his crew to do something against the enemy. But experience had taught the engineers from Mobile that trying to rush things with something as radical as a submarine boat could lead to disaster. Not only did the *Hunley* require maintenance to her internal systems, such as the propeller shaft, pumps and valves, but a suitable mooring had to be found where she could strike at the enemy. While the crew prepared the boat for action, McClintock received a letter from General Jordan, Beauregard's chief of staff:

"I am authorized to say that John Fraser & Co. will pay over to any parties who shall destroy the US Steam ironclad *Ironside* the sum of $100,000, a similar sum for the destruction of the wooden frigate *Wabash*, and the sum of $50,000 for every monitor sunk. I have reason to believe that other men of wealth will unite and give with equal munificence toward the same end. At the same time steps are being taken to secure a large sum to be settled for the support of the families of parties, who, making any attempt against the fleet now attacking our outer works, shall fail in the enterprise, and fall or be captured in the attempt."[5]

While the offer of a reward must have been tantalizing, the immediate problem was in preparing the boat, familiarizing the crew with the Charleston channels, and constructing the torpedoes. With explosive expert E. C. Singer now on the scene, orders were issued to the arsenal commander: "Charleston, S.C. August 16th 1863. Major: The commanding General desires that you will render every assistance of material and labor to Messrs. Whitney and Watson, in the construction of torpedoes to be used with their submarine vessel which he regards as the most formidable engine of war for the defense of Charleston now at his disposition."

The names of this first crew which began operations in Charleston are lost to history, although they were most probably men that had come with the *Hunley* from the Park & Lyons shop in Mobile. It is also probable that McClintock commanded, with Gus Whitney acting as second officer manning the aft ballast tank. Horace Hunley, still chaffing on detached service in Mississippi, finally arrived in Charleston on August 20.[6] In light of subsequent events, it is important to reflect upon the fact that these men were civilians, operating under military jurisdiction, who were now thrust into one of the most violent and dangerous spots of the war. Much, however, was expected of them.

From the sketchy records that are available, and by referring to a layout of Charleston harbor, it would appear that the first operations of the *Hunley* were from an area known as "The Cove," located behind Fort Moultrie at the end of Sullivan's Island. By hugging the shoreline it would have been easy to avoid the line of anchored torpedoes and gain access to the outer harbor and the open sea. Even this route, however, was fraught with many dangers, not the least of which was that if the towed contact-torpedo struck the beach it would explode.

The situation at Charleston at this time was truly desperate. Fierce duels between the Federal ironclads and Forts Moultrie and Sumter were daily occurrences. To the south, Battery Wagner on Morris Island was cut of and besieged by thousands of Federal troops who had occupied the southern portion of the island. Forty-seven heavy siege guns and mortars had been moved up to a position where they could pound Wagner into submission. By night the darkened sky was crisscrossed with streaks of light, as huge shells with their sputtering fuses sped toward their intended targets. At times, sleek, low-silhouetted block-ade runners would slip through the barrage to unload their precious cargo at the Charleston wharves.[7]

With the *Hunley* operating out of "The Cove," it was now in a posi-tion to strike at the numerous Federal warships lying offshore. During the third week of August, McClintock and his engineer crew made three nocturnal sorties against the Federal fleet but with no success. Keeping just below the surface, they propelled their invention several miles out to sea towing the deadly torpedo behind them. Rising to the surface every twenty minutes to check the heading and renew the air supply, McClintock could plainly see the enemy warships silhouetted against the darkened sky. After several moments, the key to the air box would be closed, the diving lever depressed, and once more the sub-marine would disappear beneath the dark surface. It is not known how near the *Hunley* came to success on these first excursions, but the very effort itself was truly remarkable. These pioneers, who were laboring at the crankshaft in the black and dank confines of the *Hunley* were, unknowingly, ushering in a whole new realm in naval warfare.

On August 21, Horace Hunley, having arrived in the city only the day before, submitted a requisition to the army quartermaster's de-partment "for nine gray jackets, three to be trimmed in gold braid. Cir-cumstances: that the men for whom they are ordered are on a special secret service and that it is necessary that they be clothed in Confeder-ate Army uniform."[8] It was not unlikely that had the crew of the *Hunley* been captured as civilians they would most certainly have been tried and hanged for involvement with a machine not recognized as a legiti-mate weapon of war. Many in the Victorian era considered subma-rines and underwater mines as "infernal machines" which were inhu-man in their method of attack. By clothing the men in Confederate uniforms, Hunley hoped to convey a sense of legitimacy to the method of war in which they were involved.

Fort Sumter, whose five-sided masonry walls once towered 50 feet above the entrance to Charleston harbor, was now only a pile of smoking rubble. Her feeble garrison could still command the ship chan-nel, but they could do nothing to support Battery Wagner on nearby Morris Island. The battery and its valiant defenders were now on their own. If only McClintock and his submarine boat could create a panic, the battery might yet be saved. Yet in spite of all their nightly sorties, success still eluded the volunteers from Mobile.

On the night of August 21–22, the citizens of Charleston were awakened at 1:30 a.m. by an indescribable shriek followed by a tre-mendous concussion. A 150-pound shell had exploded in the center of the city, and before dawn, fourteen more rounds had been pumped indiscriminately into the heart of Charleston. The Federal "Swamp

Angel" had announced its presence. The Union Army had secretly mounted a huge 8-inch Parrot gun on Morris Island which could throw a 200-pound shell more than four miles. This gun was not aimed at Battery Wagner or Fort Sumter; the implicit intent was to kill civilians in Charleston and level the once proud South Carolina city.

The next morning, the Charleston *Daily Courier* printed a blistering editorial under the heading, "The Bombardment!" The first paragraph stated: "The startling events that have occurred since our last issue have opened up a new chapter in the history of the war. Our ferocious foe, maddened to desperation at the heroic obstinacy and resistance to his powerful combination of land and naval forces to reduce Fort Sumter and our batteries on Morris Island, tries the horrible and brutal resort, without the usual notice, of firing, at midnight, upon the city, full of sleeping women and children, to intimidate our commanding general into a surrender of those fortifications. Our people are nerved for the crisis and with calm determination have resolved on making it a struggle for life or death."

Living in Charleston at the time was a young girl by the name of Emma Holmes, who fortunately kept a diary that has survived to this day. Her entries for that period shed new light on that frightful night: "He (General Gillmore, commanding the Union forces on Morris Island) has turned his guns against a city filled with old men, women, children, and hospitals. I think I must have woke about three o'clock. Mr. Bull called out soon after to Rosa to listen to the shelling. It was a most peculiar fearful sound—the sharp scream or whiz through the air, and they sounded exactly as if coming over the house."

"I was startled and much excited, but not frightened, but it produced a very solemn feeling. I lay with the windows partly open every moment expecting a shell might burst and kill me. I must have lain thus at least three quarters of an hour, when Rosa and Becca came down to my room so thoroughly scared they did not know what to do. I had never seen or heard of Rosa's being scared before, but this time she acknowledged she was so scared that her strength had utterly failed her, every limb ached, and she thought if she remained she would have fever."

"She declared she could not move while the shelling was going on, for she was afraid to go upstairs. Her feelings had been similar to mine. She said she did not feel fit to die, yet every moment expected death."[9]

Many now wondered why the submarine torpedo boat was not pressing its attacks more aggressively. The *H. L. Hunley* was fully operational, McClintock and Whitney were by now well-versed in its operation, and a handsome reward had been offered for the destruction of any Union warships, yet reports circulating around Charleston indicated that absolutely nothing was happening with the submarine. McClintock was no coward. To venture out six or seven miles into the dark Atlantic submerged in a manned-powered submarine required courage enough. Up to this time, however, the opportunity to destroy a Federal warship had simply not presented itself.

On August 23, Brigadier General Thomas L. Clingman, commanding on Sullivan's Island, reported to Assistant Adjutant General Captain W. F. Nance: "The torpedo boat started at sunset but returned, as they state, because of an accident. Whitney says that though McClintock is timid, yet it shall go tonight unless the weather is bad." Later that evening Nance received yet another uncomplimentary message concerning the conduct of the submarine's crew: "The torpedo boat has not gone out. I do not think it will render any service under its present management." With the sending of this last communication the fate of the *Hunley's* crew was sealed. Within twenty-four hours, the boat was seized by military authorities and turned over to the Confederate Navy. Whitney and Hunley, it appears, remained in Charleston as advisors to the navy crew, while McClintock and the men from the Park & Lyons shop returned to Mobile.[10]

Beauregard selected Lieutenant John A. Payne, CSN, to be the submarine's new commander. Payne, who was serving on the CSS *Chicora* at Charleston at the time, brought eight volunteers with him from the ironclad. The young navy lieutenant was from Alabama and had served on the CSS *Raleigh* during the two-day battle in Hampton Roads, Virginia, the previous year. After the evacuation of Norfolk by the Confederates, Payne was assigned to the Charleston Squadron, where from the very first day of the arrival of the *Hunley* from Mobile, he had taken a keen interest in the workings of the submarine.

Payne began immediately to train his crew and the *Hunley* could be seen making daily practice dives about the harbor. Considered an aggressive officer, Payne wasted little time in preparing his men for a strike against the enemy. A curious fact, however, is that this first navy crew did all of their training and practice during daylight hours, whereas any successful attack, because the trailing torpedo was easily visible during daylight hours, would have to be carried out at night. After the war, McClintock wrote about the casual way some, and by inference, Lieutenant Payne, approached the operation of the submarine: "The boat and machinery was so very simple, that many persons at first inspection believed that they could work the boat without practice, or experience, and although I endeavored to prevent inexperienced persons from going underwater in the boat, I was not always successful in preventing them." McClintock is undoubtedly referring to the impetuous Payne and his eager crew of Confederate sailors.[11]

It was at about this time that tragedy struck. On August 29, Payne and his crew had once again been making practice dives in the harbor when the lieutenant ordered his men to power the boat to the docks at nearby Fort Johnson in order to prepare for their first night excursion. Either immediately before or shortly after they had tied up to the wharf, an accident occurred that caused the boat to plunge rapidly to the murky bottom. Lieutenant Charles H. Hasker, another officer from the *Chicora* who had volunteered as part of the crew, later explained in graphic detail just what happened:

"We were lying astern of the steamer *Etowah* (*Etiwan*), near Fort Johnson, in Charleston Harbor. Lieutenant Payne, who was in charge, got fowled (sic) in the manhole by the hawser and in trying to clear himself got his foot on the lever which controlled the fins. He had just previously given the order to go ahead. The boat made a dive while the manholes were open and filled rapidly. Payne got out of the forward hole and two others out of the aft hole. Six of us went down with the boat. I had to get over the bar which connected the fins and through the manhole. This I did by forcing myself through the column of water which was rapidly filling the boat. The manhole plate came down on my back; but I worked my way out until my left leg was caught by the plate, pressing the calf of my leg in two. Held in this manner, I was carried to the bottom in 42 feet of water. When the boat touched bottom I felt the pressure relax. Stooping down I took hold of the manhole plate, drew out my wounded limb, and swam to the surface. Five men were drowned on this occasion.... I was the only man that went to the bottom with the 'Fish Boat' and came up to tell the tale."[12]

A more detailed description of the tragedy appeared in 1898 when Hasker paid a visit to Simon Lake's New Jersey home to examine the inventor's recently completed submarine boat. Hasker explained, Lake later wrote, that that they had just "parted away from the dock in tow of the gunboat *Ettawan* (*Etiwan*) by a line thrown over the hatch combing. She had been trimmed down so that she had very little freeboard, and as she gained headway she started to 'sheer' due to her peculiar flatiron-shaped bow."

"Lieutenant Payne, who was in command, attempted to throw the tow line off the hatch combing but got caught in the bight of the line. On his struggle to free himself he knocked a prop from under the tiller of the horizontal diving rudder, which had been set to hold the bow up. As soon as the prop was knocked out the tiller dropped down and inclined the horizontal rudder to dive, and the vessel dove with her hatches open."

"Lieutenant Payne freed himself, and Charles Hasker managed to get partly out of one of the hatches before the vessel sank, but the inrushing force of the water closed the hatch door, which caught him by the calf of his leg, and he was carried with the vessel to the bottom in forty-two feet of water. However, he maintained his presence of mind, and when the vessel became full it balanced the pressure so he could release himself from the hatch cover. He was a good swimmer and escaped to the surface. Two men escaped from the other hatch. The other five members of the crew were drowned in the vessel."[13]

Payne and Hasker escaped through the forward hatch while Charles L. Sprague and an unidentified seaman struggled through the rush of water coming in the aft hatch. When the exhausted Hasker broke the surface, anxious faces desperately scanned the turbulent waters expecting additional crew members to follow, but none came. There was nothing anyone could do. The *Hunley* was now resting deep in the mud under 42 feet of water. Five of her crew members, expressions of terror still frozen on their upturned faces, were sprawled over her stationary propeller shaft. Those who witnessed the tragedy were astounded at just how quickly the submarine had gone down. It had taken only a few seconds to snuff out the lives of five young Confederate sailors. Their names were Frank Doyle, John Kelly, Michael Cane, Nicholas Davis, all from the CSS *Chicora*; and Absolum Williams from the ironclad and CSS *Palmetto State*.[14]

Recent research by South Carolina State Senator Glenn McConnell indicates that these five *Hunley* crew members were interned in a cemetery for Confederate sailors and marines which was obliterated in 1947 during the construction of the Citadel's Johnson Hagood Stadium. Why the graves and markers were not moved is unknown. Plans are now under way to exhume the remains of the crewmen and rebury them with full military honors in Magnolia Cemetery.[15]

The loss of the *Hunley* and the drowning of five of her crew, which was immediately reported in the Charleston papers, had a depressing and demoralizing effect on the citizens of the city. Much had been expected from this "secret weapon," and now all hope of alleviating the relentless daily pressure from the Union forces seemed to be resting forty feet down on the muddy bottom of Charleston harbor. The saga of the *H. L. Hunley* was not about to end here, however. General Beauregard and Flag Officer Tucker decided that it was imperative that they raise the submarine, recruit another crew, and put the boat back into operation.

Within seventy-two hours of the *Hunley's* fatal plunge, negotiations had been completed for her salvage. The monumental task was assigned to two civilian divers at Charleston—Angus Smith and David Broadfoot. These two had become something of a legend in the Charleston area, having performed numerous other dives and recoveries both for the government and for private firms. The activities and successes of these two individuals are exceptionally remarkable considering the infancy and number of unknowns connected with helmeted diving during the nineteenth century. With contract in hand, Smith and Broadfoot, along with Lieutenant Payne, gathered up their gear and headed for the dock at Fort Johnson.[16]

Working only a few hundred yards from Fort Sumter, which was under continual daily bombardment, the divers found that the submarine was slowly sinking deeper and deeper into the mud. To free her, and raise her to the surface, would require heavy chains and large ships with cranes to do the lifting. At forty feet down, visibility was near zero in the pitch black water. For several days Smith and Broadfoot, pulling heavy chains behind them, tunneled under the still settling *Hunley* while the furious artillery duel between the Federal ironclads and the Confederate forts continued unabated above them.

Finally, after ten days of effort, the chains and ropes were secured and two vessels above began the slow process of winching the submarine and the five crew members out of the muck and mire that had imprisoned them. Once the *Hunley* broke the surface, hoses were dropped down her hatches and pumps started. Soon the ill-fated craft was floating well enough on its own for a steamer to tow her to the Fort Johnson wharf. There, after being tied securely to the dock, came the grisly task of removing the dead seamen. With that gruesome chore completed, Smith and Broadfoot, as part of the contract with the government, cleaned the submarine, and on September 14, had it towed to a city dock across the harbor. Although Lieutenant Payne continued in command, it appears that for the next several weeks the *Hunley* rocked gently in her slip while awaiting the authorities' decision on just what to do with her.[17]

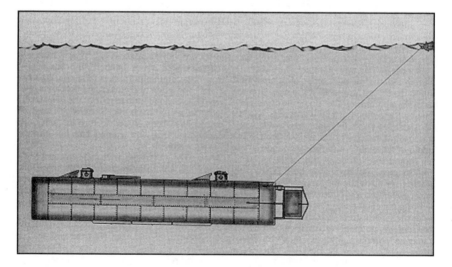

Drawing of the *Hunley* with the towed torpedo
Caldwell Whisler, courtesy of Mark K. Ragan

Lieutenant Charles H. Hasker. Hasker escaped through the forward hatch when the *Hunley* went down on August 29, 1863.

Naval Historical Center

Daniel M. Lee, a nephew of General Robert E. Lee and a midshipman on the ironclad CSS *Chicora*, helped pull Lieutenant Hasker from the waters off Fort Johnson when the *Hunley* went down.

Author's Collection

The "Swamp Angel," as it was styled, opened an indiscriminate fire on Charleston on August 22, 1863. The monstrous 8-inch Parrott cannon could fire a 200-pound projectile more than four miles. Union officers used the steeple of St. Michael's Church as their aiming point.

National Archives

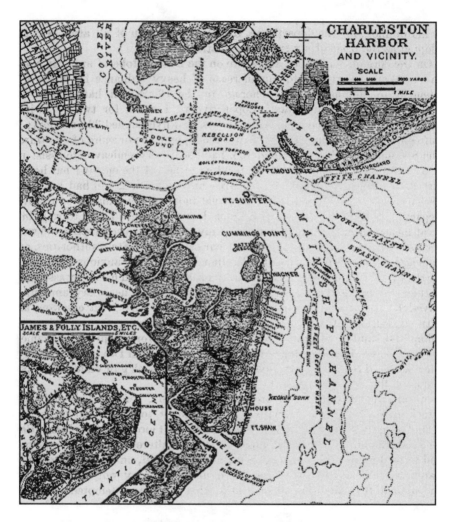

Map of the harbor at Charleston, South Carolina

Battles and Leaders

General Pierre Gustave Toutant Beauregard, Confederate military commander at Charleston, South Carolina

Library of Congress

A photograph of Fort Johnson, taken after the evacuation of Charleston in 1865
National Archives

Fort Sumter in 1862. Note the Confederate First National flag.
National Archives

Chapter Five
Disaster Strikes Again

The decision on how—if at all—to employ the submarine was formulated on the afternoon of September 19, 1863, when a letter, written by Horace Hunley, arrived at Beauregard's headquarters. By this time the Federals had completed their investment of Morris Island; Battery Wagner had been abandoned by the Confederates on the night of September 6; and downtown Charleston, still under heavy bombardment, was becoming a ghost town. Something had to be done to strike back at the powerful Union forces. Hunley's letter provided an option:

"Charleston, September 19th, 1863. General P. G. T. Beauregard Sir. I am part owner of the torpedo boat the *Hunley*. I have been interested in building this description of boat since the beginning of the war, and furnished the means entirely of building the predecessor of this boat, which was lost in an attempt to blow up a Federal vessel off Fort Morgan in Mobile Harbor. I feel therefore a deep interest in its success. I propose, if you will place the boat in my hands, to furnish a crew (in whole or in part) from Mobile who are well acquainted with its management and make the attempt to destroy a vessel of the enemy as early as practicable. Very respectfully your servant, H. L. Hunley."[1]

Hunley, who may have had a hand in the recovery of the boat, seems to have had little reservation about putting it back into service.

His offer to provide a crew indicates his belief that most of the men from Mobile who had operated the boat under McClintock would most likely be willing to return and serve under him. Considering the deteriorating situation at Charleston and the urgent need to strike a blow at the invading Federal forces, Beauregard and Tucker jumped at the opportunity to place the *Hunley* back in operation. It appears, however, that the government insisted that a military officer be in command of the boat, with Hunley exercising logistical control. With this understanding in mind, Hunley communicated with his friends back at the Park and Lyons shop in Mobile.

Beauregard ordered the submarine cleaned and repaired, while Hunley waited for the arrival of his crew from Mobile. William Alexander, writing forty years after the war, recorded for posterity the names of these men:

"General Beauregard then turned the craft over to a volunteer crew from Mobile known as the 'Hunley and Parks crew.' Captain Hunley and Thomas Parks (one of the best of men), of the firm Park & Lyons, in whose shop the boat had been built, were in charge, with Brockband, Patterson, McHugh, Marshall, White, Beard, and another (Dixon) as the crew. Until the day this crew left Mobile, it was understood that I was to be one of them, but at the last moment Mr. Parks prevailed on me to let him take my place. Nearly all of the men had some experience in the boat before leaving Mobile, and were well qualified to operate her."[2]

Sometime during the first week of October 1863, the crew from Mobile arrived in Charleston. With the submarine now in excellent condition, they wasted little time in refreshing themselves with her operations. Lieutenant Dixon was at the helm, with Thomas Park (son of Mr. Park of Park & Lyons) serving as second officer at the aft ballast tank. Robert Brockband (some records spell his name Brockbank), Joseph Patterson, Charles McHugh, John Marshall, Henry Beard, and Charles Sprague (the only member of Lieutenant Payne's crew to remain with the boat) took their assigned positions at the propeller crank. With the *Hunley* once again in the hands of an experienced crew, she was soon observed practicing her torpedo runs by diving under the various Confederate warships in the harbor.

By October 10, Dixon and his crew felt confident enough to begin nightly sorties against the Union ironclads and blockaders lying offshore. Two last minute requisitions called for a new compass and a fresh tow-rope for the trailing torpedo. With these items in place, it was now only a matter of waiting for the right weather and sea conditions.

Five days later, on the gray, overcast morning of October 15, 1863, those conditions had not yet materialized, therefore it was decided to make a few more practice runs in the harbor. For some unknown reason, which is a mystery to this day, Dixon was not present that morning, and Hunley determined to command the boat himself. It is probable that he had controlled the boat on some of the dives at Mobile, therefore he was not totally unfamiliar with her operation. After the crew had squeezed through the forward and aft hatches, Hunley took his place at the helm, and Park stood ready at the aft ballast tank and sea cock. When the heavy hatch covers were swung shut and bolted from inside, little did the confident crew suspect that it would be the last time they would ever see the light of day.

What really transpired within the dark confines of the *Hunley's* hull that gray, rainy day in October will never really be known. Eyewitnesses, standing on the Cooper River, numerous docks, and the receiving ship CSS *Indian Chief*, reported observing the submarine making its usual practice run with nothing apparently amiss. The first dive was under the *Indian Chief* itself. Sailors on board the receiving ship watched as the *Hunley* approached from the starboard side, and when approximately 100 yards out, the diving planes were depressed, and the boat disappeared beneath the surface. Those not on duty casually strolled to the port side of the *Indian Chief* and waited for the boat to surface on the other side. After several minutes had gone by, it slowly became apparent that something dreadful had happened.

An extract in the *Navy Official Records* taken from the Journal of Operations, kept at Confederate headquarters in Charleston, sheds some light on the tragedy:

"October 15, 1863.—Raining again this morning, and too hazy to get a report of the fleet."

"Today was exceedingly quiet, and the enemy did not fire a single shot, although Batteries Simkins and Cheves were in slow action, the former firing 33 rounds and the latter 10 rounds."

"An unfortunate accident occurred this morning with the submarine boat, by which Captain H. L. Hunley and 7 men lost their lives in an attempt to run under the navy receiving ship. The boat left the wharf at 9:25 a.m. and disappeared at 9:35. As soon as she sunk air bubbles were seen to rise to the surface of the water, and from this fact it is supposed the hole in the top of the boat by which the men entered, was not properly closed. It was impossible at the time to make any effort to rescue the unfortunate men, as the water was some 9 fathoms deep."[3]

From General Beauregard we find: "Lieutenant Dixon made repeated descents in the harbor of Charleston, diving under the naval receiving ship which lay at anchor there. But one day when he was absent from the city, Mr. Hunley, unfortunately, wishing to handle the boat himself, made the attempt. It was readily submerged, but did not rise again to the surface, and all on board perished from asphyxiation."[4]

Once again the salvage team of Smith and Broadfoot was called into action. On the day following the disappearance of the submarine, the two underseas divers began probing the murky waters beneath the keel of the receiving ship *Indian Chief*. On October 17, the following request was submitted to Flag Officer Tucker: "Captain Angus Smith engaged in raising the submarine torpedo boat which was unfortunately sunk a few days ago, requires the assistance of several boats and crews to endeavor to raise the vessel. I therefore request that you will give him the necessary aid in this matter, and also that the receiving ship under which the torpedo boat is thought to lie, may be moved from it's present position, so as not to interfere with the operations of dragging for the boat."

With the request granted, and the *Indian Chief* moved away from the search area, the following entry was entered the next day in the Journal of Operations: "Oct. 18th, Mr. Smith provided with submarine armor, found the sunken submarine boat today in 9 fathoms of water. The engineering department was instructed to furnish Mr. Smith all facilities in the way of ropes, chains, etc., that an attempt might be made to recover the boat."[5]

Within hours of the discovery of the sunken craft, a severe weather front moved through the Charleston area, postponing salvage operations for several days. Finally, with the weather clearing, Smith and Broadfoot were able to descend the fifty-six feet to where they had first sighted the sunken hull. To their amazement they found the *Hunley* with her prowl buried deep in the mud, and her propeller pointing toward the surface at approximately thirty degrees. It appeared as though the boat had literally dived straight to the bottom. There was no hole in the boat, the hatches were closed, and the ballast weights, designed to be released in case of an emergency, were still attached to the keel.

Once again the hardworking team of Smith and Broadfoot snaked their heavy chains and ropes under the submarine, and soon large floating cranes lifted her to the surface. Placed this time on a dock at the foot of Calhoun Street, the hatches were pried open. General Beauregard, who seems to have been present, remembered that awful moment: "When the boat was discovered, raised and opened, the spectacle was indescribably ghastly; the unfortunate men were contorted into all kinds of horrible attitudes; some clutching candles, evidently endeavoring to force open the man-holes; others lying in the bottom tightly grappled together, and the blackened faces of all presented the expression of their despair and agony."[6]

Writing from memory many years after the war, Lieutenant William Alexander has left the most concise analysis of what probably happened that rainy day in the dark waters beneath the *Indian Chief*. Even though he was in Mobile at the time, he later became extremely familiar with the *Hunley,* and was in the best position to evaluate just what might have happened.

"The position in which the boat was found on the bottom of the river," he wrote, "the condition of the apparatus discovered after it was raised and pumped out, and the position of the bodies in the boat, furnished a full explanation for her loss. The boat, when found, was lying on the bottom at an angle of about 35 degrees, the bow deep in the mud. The bolting-down bolts of each cover had been removed. When the hatch covers were lifted considerable air and gas escaped. Captain Hunley's body was forward, with his head in the forward hatchway, his right hand on top of his head (he had been trying, it would seem, to raise the hatch cover). In his left hand was a candle that had never been lighted, the sea-cock on the forward end, or 'Hunley's' ballast tank, was wide open, the cock wrench not on the plug, but lying on the bottom of the boat. Mr. Park's body was found with his head in the after hatchway, his right hand above his head. He also had been trying to raise the hatch cover, but the pressure was too great. The sea-cock to his tank was properly closed, and the tank was nearly empty. The other bodies were floating in the water. Hunley and Parks were undoubtedly asphyxiated, the others drowned. The bolts that had held the iron keel ballast had been partly turned, but not sufficient to release it."

"In the light of these conditions, we can easily depict before our minds, and almost readily explain, what took place in the boat during the moments immediately following its submergence. Captain Hunley's practice with the boat had made him quite familiar and expert in handling her, and this familiarity produced at this time forgetfulness. It was found in practice to be easier on the crew to come to the surface by giving the pumps a few strokes and ejecting some of the water ballast, than by the momentum of the boat operating on the elevated fins. At this time the boat was under way, lighted through the dead-lights in the hatchways. He partly turned the fins to go down, but thought, no doubt, that he needed more ballast and opened his sea cock. Immediately the boat was in total darkness. He then undertook to light the candle. While trying to do this the tank quietly flooded, and under great pressure the boat sank very fast and soon overflowed, and the first intimation they would have of anything being wrong was the water rising fast, but noiselessly, about their feet in the bottom of the boat. They tried to release the iron keel ballast, but did not turn the keys quite far enough, therefore failed. The water soon forced the air to the top of the boat and into the hatchways, where captains Hunley and Parks were found. Parks had pumped his ballast tank dry, and no doubt

Captain Hunley had exhausted himself on his pump, but he had forgotten that he had not closed his sea-cock."[7]

Horace Hunley may not have been as "familiar" with the boat as Alexander alleges. If Hunley had been able at any time to close the sea cock and stop the flow of water into the forward ballast tank, the crew probably could have bailed the water from the bottom of the hull back into the tank where it could have been pumped out. When the boat struck bottom, whether from inattention or miscalculation of the depth, the handle to the valve must have been jarred off and fell to the bottom of the forward compartment. In the pitch blackness and confusion that followed the heavy jolt, the wrench could not be found. As the frigid water began to spill over the top of the forward tank and fill the darkened hull, the men scrambled toward the upraised stern hoping that Park could force his hatch open. But at a depth of more than fifty feet the outside pressure was too great and they must have soon realized that there would be no escape. Beneath nine fathoms of water, the bow of their boat firmly stuck in the mud and water rising rapidly about them, their desperate cries for help were soon silenced by the cold waters of Charleston harbor.

On November 8, 1863, the remains of Horace Hunley and his brave crew were laid to rest with full military honors, in Magnolia Cemetery on the banks of the beautiful Cooper River. From a letter received in New Orleans by Hunley's sister shortly after the funeral, we catch a faint glimpse of this sad event:

"Mrs. V. W. Barrow, New Orleans, Louisiana. Madam: It becomes my painful duty to address you in relation to the decease of your brother Horace Lawson Hunley. He had delegated me at Mobile to come to Charleston, S. C. I started and arrived on the 18th of October. He was drowned on the 15th three days previous. I immediately telegraphed Mr. Leovy and other of his friends."

"Mr. Leovy came to Charleston and remained a few days. It took several days to make arrangements to raise the boat to enable us to produce the bodies. When the raising tackle and hoisting boats were ready, a strong north east wind blew for many days. We could not work at the raising of the boat, only in smooth weather and slack water of the tide, therefore the great delay."

"We succeeded in raising the boat and recovered the body of Captain Hunley on Saturday evening, the 7th of November. I had a fine lined coffin ready. The funeral took place on Sunday the 8th at four o'clock p.m. General Beauregard ordered a military escort, two companies and a band of music. The funeral service was solemn and impressive, performed by the Rev. W. B. Yates, Episcopal. On Sunday evening the remaining seven bodies were recovered, and on Monday I had them buried with funeral services by the same clergyman and in a lot adjoining the one of Captain Hunley. I then selected a tombstone, it is small but appropriate, merely to mark the place, with the following inscription: 'Captain Horace Lawson Hunley, aged 39 years. A native of Tennessee, but for many years a citizen of New Orleans, who lost his life in the service of his country.'"

"At the grave I could not refrain from tears as the casket of the spirit of a noble and generous man was being lowered, 'earth to earth,' to its final resting place. I lost in him my best friend. My wife had also become much attached to him. He was so gentlemanly and kind. When I came home and related the death and burial, she wept though it had been a dear relative. And said, 'Oh! That I could have been with you to have wept at the grave for an only sister whose heart must bleed for a brother lost and buried among strangers.' But here I assure you, (he was) not without friends, for he was beloved by all who knew him. I remain Madam, very respectfully, Gardner Smith."[8]

**Captain John R. Tucker, commander of the
Charleston Squadron**
Scharf's History of the Confederate States Navy

**Brigadier General Thomas Jordan, chief of
staff to General Beauregard**
Miller's Photographic History

Federal heavy guns continue to pound the city of Charleston.
Frank Leslie's *The American Soldier in the Civil War*

The grave of Horace L. Hunley in Magnolia Cemetery, Charleston, South Carolina
Photo by the author

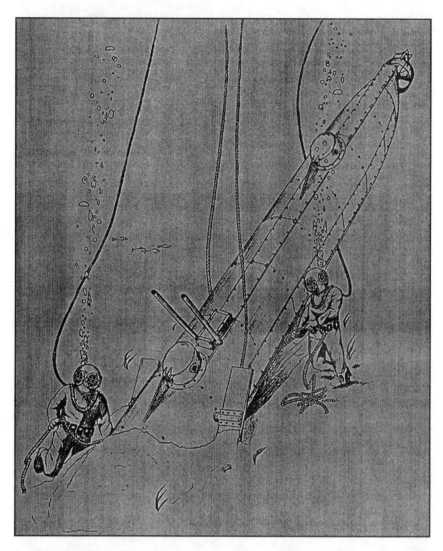

Artist's concept of Angus Smith and David Broadfoot working on raising the *Hunley* **after she had plowed into the mud, killing Horace Hunley and seven other crew members**

Greg Cottrell, courtesy of Mark K. Ragan

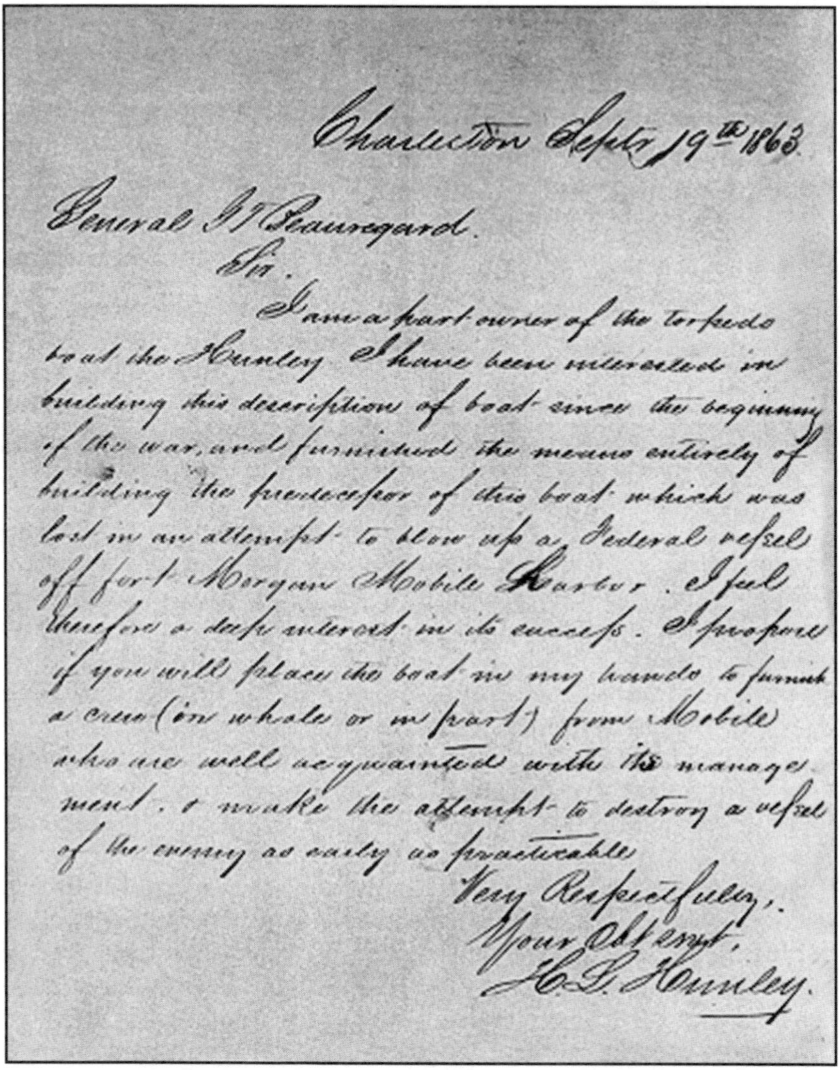

Hunley's letter to General P. G. T. Beauregard

Chapter Six
Dixon Takes Command

During the period of time that Smith and Broadfoot were struggling to free the *Hunley* from the mud of Charleston harbor, Lieutenant Dixon and Henry Dillingham, an agent for the Confederate Army, traveled to Mobile. There at the Park & Lyons shop the hammers and saws fell silent as Dixon conveyed the sad news of the death of Hunley and seven of their closest comrades. Pulling his good friend William Alexander aside, Dixon revealed his real reason for returning to Mobile. He had been given specific authority, he said, to recruit another crew from the mechanics of the machine shop. In spite of the tragic news which had been conveyed to them, Alexander and two others immediately volunteered to accompany Dixon back to Charleston.

Upon their return, Dixon and Alexander faced the formidable task of convincing General Beauregard to allow them to continue to operate the dangerous craft. The commanding general, after the loss of Horace Hunley and his seven men, had lost confidence in the submarine and refused to allow anyone to operate her. After many hours of discussion, Beauregard finally acquiesced to the arguments of the persuasive Dixon and placed the boat in his care, stipulating that it was not to be submerged, but to be kept only on the surface. Ample evidence exists, however, that once the *Hunley* was back in operation this provision was ignored.[1]

With the boat now completely under his command, Dixon wrote the following letter to General Jordan:

"Charleston, November the 14th, 1863. Brig. General Jordan, Chief of Staff, Sir: Before I can proceed with my work of cleaning the Sub-Marine boat, I shall have to request of you an order on the Quarter-master or Engineer Department for ten Negroes, also an order on the Commissary Department for soap, brushes, and lime, and an order on the Arsenal to have some work done at that place. In order to make all possible haste with this work, I would be pleased to have those orders granted at your earliest convenience. I am Yours with Respect Lt. Geo. E. Dixon, Commanding Sub-Marine Boat."[2]

With the *Hunley* having spent approximately three months in the water plus several weeks on the bottom of Charleston harbor, it was essential that she be given a complete refurbishing. The large number of men requested were used to hoist the submarine out of the water, and soon it was resting on the Mount Pleasant wharf. (It was while on this dock that Conrad Wise Chapman, a local Charleston artist, painted the now famous portrait of the *Hunley*.) With the boat now out of the water, it would have been an easy task to repack all of the stuffing boxes that sealed the various rods and shafts that passed through the hull.

With the boat cleaned, painted, and resealed, Dixon and Alexander now made another trip to the commanding general's headquarters. "After many refusals and much discussion," Alexander wrote, "General Beauregard finally assented to our going aboard the Confederate States Navy receiving ship *Indian Chief*, then lying in the river, and secure volunteers for a crew, strictly enjoining upon us, however, that a full history of the boat in the past,...and full explanation of the hazardous nature of the service required of them, was to be given to each man."[3]

Going on board the *Indian Chief*, Dixon and Alexander, careful to comply with the stipulations of General Beauregard, explained the hazardous nature of the duty that men would find if they volunteered as a member of the submarine's crew. According to Alexander: "We had no difficulty in getting volunteers to man her. I don't believe a man considered the danger which awaited him. The honor of being the first to engage the enemy in this novel way overshadowed all else."[4] Dixon selected five of the most able-bodied seamen, for the rigors of powering the boat perhaps hours at a time was extremely strenuous and only the strongest men would do.

The five Confederate sailors selected that day were: Seaman Joseph Ridgeway, Seaman C. F. Simkins, Seaman Frank J. Collins, Seaman Arnold Becker, and Boatswain's Mate James A. Wicks.[5] Only five men were needed, for, as previously stated, in addition to Dixon and

Alexander, two men had volunteered from the Park & Lyons machine shop in Mobile. Unfortunately, records are frustratingly incomplete, but it is thought that the name of one of these two machinists from Mobile was White.[6]

With the crew now complete, serious training could begin. Dixon gathered his men at the Mount Pleasant dock where the *Hunley* sat resting high and dry on her cradle. With the boat out of the water it was an easy task to familiarize them with all of the intricate details and workings of the submarine. One can picture the expressions of wonder and excitement as the men squeezed through the narrow hatchways and took their assigned places at the propeller crank. Once on board, Dixon would have explained the workings of the compass, control wheel, ballast tanks, and pumps. Moving the diving lever up and down, he would have explained the function of the diving planes on the outside of the hull, and how the mercury gauge was used to maintain a desired depth below the surface. Next the men would have been told to turn the long gray crankshaft, which should have been an easy task with no resistance on the propeller. It is almost comical, now, to imagine the *Hunley* sitting on the dock with her three-bladed propeller spinning madly.

Soon the *Hunley* was returned to the cold, green waters of Charleston harbor. Now the real training could begin. The first excursion with the refurbished submarine was probably a short cruise on the water's surface about the harbor to allow the men to gain confidence in their craft. It was not long, however, before Dixon was making practice runs on Confederate warships nearby. A Confederate deserter from the Charleston Squadron later reported to Federal authorities that he "saw her go under the *Indian Chief*, and then saw her go back again. She made about one-half mile in the dives. Saw her dive under the *Charleston*; went under about 250 feet from her, and came up about 300 feet beyond her. Was about twenty minutes under the water when she went under the *Indian Chief.*"[7]

The *Hunley's* commander and his men were now ready. Putting on their best dress uniforms, Dixon and Alexander again reported to General Beauregard's headquarters. Immediately after their visit, Confederate military headquarters issued the following order:

"Charleston, S. C., December 14, 1863, Special Orders, Number 271. First Lieut. George E. Dixon, Twenty-first Regiment Alabama Volunteers, will take command and direction of the Submarine Torpedo-Boat 'H. L. Hunley,' and proceed tonight to the mouth of the harbor, or as far as capacity of the vessel will allow, and will sink and destroy any vessel of the enemy with which he can come in conflict."

"All officers of the Confederate army in this department are commanded, and all naval officers are requested, to give such assistance to

Lieutenant Dixon in the discharge of his duties as may be practicable, should he apply therefor. By command of General Beauregard."[8]

The remainder of that day was spent in anxious activity as the crew checked and double checked the workings of their submarine. This would be the first time that the *Hunley* had ventured past the crumbling walls of Fort Sumter and into the open sea since August when James McClintock was in command. After sundown, with the location of the currents and sandbars marked on their charts and stowed aboard the submarine, Dixon ordered his men to board and take their places. This first mission against the strong Union fleet, lying outside the bar, was probably fraught with mistakes and miscalculations as most first-time sorties are.

During some of the trials, Dixon had noticed the problems with the towed torpedo that Alexander had pointed out in Mobile. Ocean currents would sometimes push the torpedo uncomfortably close to the submarine. As though the erratic behavior of the deadly torpedo was not enough, the *Hunley* had to contend with numerous other obstacles, such as strong currents that could send the boat miles off course, shifting sandbars, enemy picket boats, and brilliant calcium lights which the Federals had erected that could light up whole areas of the ocean. To reach the enemy ironclads offshore, Dixon found that it was extremely taxing on the crew to crank the submarine all the way from the Mount Pleasant dock to several miles out to sea. In the future, arrangements would have to be made to have the *Hunley* towed by a steam vessel to some point just past Fort Sumter in order to lessen the fatigue on the men at the crankshaft.

Needless to say this first nocturnal sortie was unsuccessful, but many valuable lessons were learned that would be applied to future missions. Dixon's first priority, after returning from their unsuccessful patrol, was to arrange for a tow on future missions. Again, the young lieutenant reported to army headquarters to present his request, and in turn was directed to seek out Chief Engineer James H. Tombs, skipper of the small torpedo boat, CSS *David*. Tombs had been given command of the torpedo boat shortly after the partially successful attack against the USS *New Ironsides* on October 5, 1863. The *David* was fifty feet in length, steam-driven, and carried her torpedo on a long spar attached to her bow.

Flag Officer John R. Tucker, commanding the Charleston Squadron, ordered Tombs to assist the *Hunley* and soon towing operations began. The plan was to tow the submarine, weather permitting, one to two miles out to sea where the towline would be cast off, and the *David* would proceed on her own sortie or return to the harbor. From that point, the *Hunley* was on her own.

A typical sortie would begin after darkness had settled on the harbor. As the cold December winds whistled over the Mount Pleasant wharf, Dixon and his crew would hurry to board their small submarine where they would wait for the arrival of the *David* torpedo boat. Once on board the boat, Dixon and Alexander, after checking to see that the inlet valves were properly closed, would make several throws on the ballast tank pump handles to ensure that the tanks were empty. With the arrival of the *David*, the towline was attached and a sharp lurch indicated that the tow had commenced. With nothing to do for the next hour or so, the *Hunley's* crew could now sit back and relax while trying not to think about the dangers ahead. As the two strange-looking craft proceeded slowly toward the outer entrance to the harbor, Alexander stood in the aft hatch squinting his eyes in the darkness trying to keep the deadly trailing torpedo in sight. Up front, his eyes glued to the glistening towline attached to the straining *David*, Dixon stood with his head and shoulders out of the forward hatch. Occasionally, the *Hunley's* commander would make slight changes to the helm in order to keep the boat directly behind the *David*.

Soon the shattered walls of Fort Sumter became plainly visible against the starry sky, and Dixon stooped down below the forward hatch to report on their progress. The nervous laughter and meaningless banter of the crew fell silent. It would not be long before the hatch covers would swing shut, and their very lives would be in the hands of the young army lieutenant at the forward hatch. Many of the men closed their eyes in quiet prayer, asking that God's protective hand would be on them this night and that this infernal war would soon end. After another thirty minutes or so, the soft vibrations of the *David's* steam engine, which could be felt through the iron hull of the submarine, slowed as the torpedo boat prepared to set the *Hunley* free. With a wave and a silent thank you, Dixon leaned out of the forward hatch and slipped the tow rope into the sea.

Stepping below, he and Alexander quietly closed the hatches and bolted them tightly shut. Lighting the candle, Dixon placed it on a shelf where its flickering glow would illuminate the compass and mercury depth gauge. The inlet valves were opened and cold sea water began surging into the ballast tanks. Soon, only the two conning towers were above the surface and the valves were closed. Dixon checked the heading on the compass, grasped the lever to hold the diving planes steady, and gave the command to put the boat under way. With a terrific release of nervous energy, eight men grasped the cold iron of the crankshaft and turned with all of their might, sending an eerie squeal throughout the dimly lit hull. The *Hunley* fairly leaped ahead as the propeller bit into the cold Atlantic. With the lethal torpedo following in her wake, the CSS *H. L. Hunley* once again set out to do battle with the unsuspecting enemy ironclads.

After several of these nightly sorties, it was learned that the Federals had deployed an elaborate system of chain booms around their ironclads which, in addition to being very dangerous for the submarine, most surely would explode the torpedo prematurely. In spite of this, Dixon continued his nightly missions into early January 1864, still being towed past Fort Sumter by the torpedo boat *David*. On one night, both the *Hunley* and the *David* came quite near meeting disaster. At some point in the tow, the *David* stopped for an unknown reason, and the *Hunley's* torpedo came drifting up alongside; the line becoming entangled in the torpedo boat's rudder assembly. Tombs and Dixon watched in horror as the glistening black explosive canister, its sides bristling with percussion contacts, drifted closer and closer. The torpedo scraped against the side of the *David's* wooden hull and everyone held their breath. A crewman from the torpedo boat dived into the icy water, untangled the lines, and pushed the torpedo away. It was a near miracle that both boats were not blown out of the water.

This would be the *Hunley's* last tow. Tombs later recounted that after submitting his report, Commander Tucker refused to allow the *David* to be put at further risk and canceled the towing operations. Dixon believed that it was just as well, for with the enemy ironclads now protected by heavy chain barriers, they would have to turn their attention to the wooden vessels of the blockading fleet which were farther out to sea. To reach them, the *Hunley* would need to move her base of operations to a point closer to the open ocean. After much searching, Dixon settled on Battery Marshall at the northern tip of Sullivan's Island as a suitable mooring for the boat. From an area known as the Back Bay, it was only a short distance through Breach Inlet to the open sea.[9]

Because the *Hunley* would be attacking wooden ships instead of ironclads, the method of attack had to be changed. The floating torpedo on a towline was discarded, and a twenty-two-foot iron pipe, similar to the wooden spar utilized by the torpedo boat *David*, was mounted on the bow. There is convincing evidence that this method of attack had been provided for all along. The painting done by Conrad Wise Chapman, on December 2, 1863, while the *Hunley* was sitting on the Mount Pleasant dock, clearly shows the spindle for the lanyard that would explode the spar torpedo—cocked off to one side so as not to interfere with the diving planes.

The torpedo now employed by the *Hunley* was unique and designed for use against wooden ships. Writing in the *U.S. Navy Proceedings* in 1937, Lieutenant Harry Von Kolnitz, USN, gives us an excellent description of how this weapon was designed to work: "A torpedo was designed which could be mounted on a short pole and which would delay its explosion until the attacking vessel could back off to a safe position. It consisted of a steel head which fitted as a thimble over the end of the twenty foot spar or pipe projecting from the bow. This was driven into the enemy's wooden hull by ramming and was retained there by saw-toothed corrugations when the fish boat backed off. As it slipped off the spar, it would keep with it the torpedo, which was a simple copper can of powder fitted with a trigger. This trigger was attached to a cord lanyard carried on a reel on deck and after the boat had backed a safe distance, 150 feet, the rope was to tighten and would trip the trigger."[10]

As the cold nights of January gave way to the equally frigid ones of February, Dixon continued to train his crew by day and undertake nightly sorties whenever the weather permitted. During this time the men were still quartered at Mount Pleasant, which required a long hike every day to reach the area behind Battery Marshall where the *Hunley* was moored. In succinct fashion, Alexander described their daily routine:

"Leave Mount Pleasant about 1 p.m., walk seven miles to Battery Marshall on the beach (this exposed us to fire, but it was the best walking), take the boat out and practice the crew for two hours in the Back bay. Dixon and myself would then stretch out on the beach with the compass between us and get the bearings of the nearest vessel as she took up her position for the night; ship up the torpedo on the boom, and, when dark, go out, steering for the vessel, proceed until the condition of the men, sea, tide, wind, moon, and daylight compelled our return to the dock: unship the torpedo, put it under guard at Battery Marshall, walk back to quarters at Mount Pleasant, and cook breakfast."[11]

It would not be long now, before glorious success would most certainly crown the efforts of Dixon and his men—but at what price?

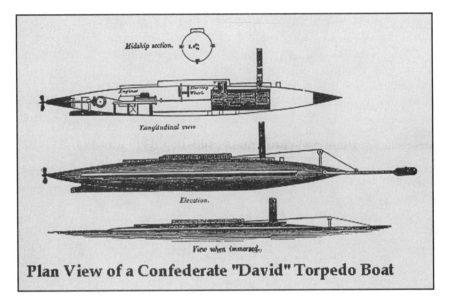

Plan View of a Confederate "David" Torpedo Boat

The *David* class torpedo boats had ballast tanks which allowed them to partially submerge.

Official Records Navy

Ruins of downtown Charleston, South Carolina

National Archives

A Confederate torpedo boat found lying in the mud after the evacuation of
Charleston in 1865. From recorded descriptions, this may be the original *David*
that provided some of the tows for the *H. L. Hunley*.

National Archives

December 2, 1863. The CSS *H.L. Hunley* on the dock where she was placed after
the death of Hunley and his crew.

Conrad Wise Chapman

The Charleston Hotel. Dixon and Alexander probably stayed here until the move to Battery Marshall.

National Archives

74

74

This may be a photo of Lieutenant George E. Dixon. The tintype was found tucked behind the cover of a photo album belonging to Queenie Bennett, Dixon's sweetheart in Alabama. It closely matches the description of him given by his commanding officer.

Courtesy of Mark K. Ragan

Chapter Seven

The *Hunley* at Breach Inlet

"As the flickering light from numerous camp fires started to appear behind the sloping walls of Battery Marshall, the crew of the *Hunley* could be seen preparing their submarine for that first night that lay ahead of them far out to sea. At the bow of the vessel, Dixon and Alexander checked the reel and line that would trip the trigger of the torpedo, making absolutely sure that nothing could accidentally snag the cord and detonate the device while it was still attached to the spar. Nearby, Seaman Becker and Collins, formally of the CSS *Indian Chief*, stamped their feet on the dock trying to keep warm while talking to some soldiers from Battery Marshall who had come over to wish them luck."

"While the last faint rays of sunlight slowly disappeared behind the distant church steeples of Charleston, Dixon asked Seaman Ridgeway to open the hatches and make ready for the rest of the crew to enter. As the young sailor stepped onto the *Hunley's* slick iron hull, the submarine gently bobbed and rolled under his weight. While reaching down to pull open the heavy hatch cover, he requested a lantern from one of his comrades. As he climbed down into the cold clammy interior of the submarine, he noticed that the flickering light given off by the small flame shimmered on the thin streaks of ice that covered the walls."

"While Alexander talked to Dixon at the bow, Wicks passed four or five canteens of water down through the rear hatch to Ridgeway, along with some hardtack and dried beef. Because the submarine would remain at sea until dawn, food and water were very important in helping the men get through the long winter night. As the crew slowly started to climb down into the cramped, icy hull, a distant boom from Morris Island notified everyone that the new batteries recently mounted on the point had come to life for their evening harassment of Charleston. As Dixon squeezed through the narrow hatch, he found the rest of the crew already at their stations talking softly amongst themselves. Wicks was saying something about his wife, Catherine, and their four daughters. The oldest daughter, Eliza, was just eleven years old. By now, the ceiling around the forward hatch would have been blackened with soot from the dozens of candles that had been burned there. The floor of the hull beneath the tarnished compass that had been sold to them by Broadfoot would be speckled with small piles of melted wax that had run down the bulkhead."

"While the crew prepared themselves for the long night that lay ahead, Dixon lit one of the candles he had brought on board and wiped the frost from the view ports and mercury gauge with an old rag."

"At the rear hatch, Alexander lifted the lantern through the narrow opening and handed it to a soldier who stood nearby. As he squeezed through the small opening and took his place at the rear ballast tank pump, Dixon asked if every one was ready. In the shadowy candle light he at once saw each man nodding yes to his question. Within moments the order to move forward was given. As the long cold propeller shaft started turning in the capable hands of Dixon's crew, our young engineering officer stood with his head above the hatch rim, steering his submarine toward the open sea and the twinkling lights of the Union fleet that lay at anchor several miles offshore...."

"All through the long cold night at sea, the crew would most certainly have been in a constant state of paranoia. Each of the many surfacings for air would have caused great uncertainty; if an enemy picket boat spotted them as they opened their hatch for air, a well-placed shot from anyone of her small deck guns would send the *Hunley* to the bottom forever. If the line to the torpedo accidentally snagged on a piece of driftwood and pulled the detonating trigger, the explosion from 90 pounds of gunpowder in front of the bow could easily rip open the hull of their vessel. From the time that the men took their places until the following dawn, nothing could be seen but the dripping condensation running down the *Hunley's* dark iron walls. During the monotony of the long night, one can only wonder as to how many times each man must have contemplated the tragic history of the diving machine, as cold and fatigue started to numb their bodies. While

Dixon knelt in front of the candle monitoring the dimly lit compass, trying to keep his submarine on course, the rest of the crew continued to turn the crankshaft hour after hour in near total darkness."

"After traveling offshore for several hours, Dixon would have checked his pocket watch for the time. With only five hours till sunrise it was decided that the *Hunley* would surface for one final observation. If no enemy ships were spotted nearby, he would rest his tired crew before starting the long journey back to Breach Inlet. As he slowly pulled back the lever connected to the forward diving planes, the narrow hatch of the submarine gently rose above the surface. Quickly he blew out the candle and wiped the condensation from the view ports for a quick look around. It was pitch black in all directions. As his weary crew continued to turn the shaft, Dixon began pumping out the forward ballast tank. He ordered Alexander at the rear of the vessel to do the same with the aft tank. As the water from both tanks was pumped back into the sea, the iron hull of the *Hunley* slowly rose in the water until her deck was several inches above the surface."

"Immediately Dixon pushed open his heavy hatch cover and scanned the horizon for any sign of an enemy picket boat. As he brought his telescope to his eye, he could see the lights of an enemy frigate twinkling through the light fog a mile and a half in front of them. From the south, about three quarters of a mile away, he could make out the faint beam of a calcium light, scanning the dark water from a picket boat. With no hostile ships in the area, Dixon ordered Alexander to stop cranking, open his hatch, and light some candles. With this order, the crew ceased cranking and took a much needed rest. With no apparent danger lurking nearby, and a cool breeze passing through the hull between the two open hatches, the mood of the crew quickly changed as canteens of water and parcels of food were passed between the men. While the crew talked and joked in the now well lit cabin, Dixon and Alexander stood in the hatches whispering between themselves while watching the dim light of the picket boat that lay to the south."

"As the *Hunley* slowly drifted in the gentle current, Dixon stood with his head above the hatch rim taking a much needed breath of fresh air. He peered at the faraway lights of an enemy frigate as he reached over to check the line in the reel, making sure that nothing had jarred or snagged it's mechanism. While his weary crew talked and rested, Dixon noticed a faint flash of lightning over the horizon. He knew from past experience that a rainstorm would severely hinder his visibility, and winds may cause the surface of the water to become too turbulent for any sort of sighting at all. Without proper sightings they could not safely find their way back. With this disturbing thought in mind, he advised his crew that, considering the weather and the distance they still had to the nearest enemy ship, they had best return to shore."

"With his crew now refreshed and ready to continue their duties, he ordered the crankshaft to once again be turned. As the iron shaft once more spun inside its metal braces, Dixon turned the forward wheel, which caused the rudder to turn to starboard. As the needle on the compass slowly came to bare on the proper heading, he straightened the wheel and told the crew to stop for a moment. At once, all the candles were blown out except Dixon's. With the bow of the *Hunley* now pointing towards Sullivan's Island, Dixon ordered the hatches sealed and Alexander to open the rear ballast tank sea valve. As the submarine slowly settled beneath the dark surface, Dixon held his candle to the view-port to monitor the water level through the thick glass pane. When the hull was seen to be three inches below the surface, both sea valves were closed and the submarine ordered to get underway. With a slight push on the heavy diving planes, the submarine once again disappeared into the sea. With the sun rising in about five hours, Dixon hoped he could guide his tiny vessel back to Breach Inlet before the dawn found him still in enemy waters."

"From Alexander's post-war writings, we are informed in vivid detail as to the many dangers faced by the crew of the *Hunley* during those cold January nights in 1864:

> It was Winter, therefore necessary that we go out with the ebb and come in with the flood tide, a fair wind and a dark moon. This latter was essential to success, as our experience had fully demonstrated the necessity of occasionally coming to the surface, slightly lifting the after hatch-cover and letting in a little air. On several occasions we came to the surface for air, opened the cover and heard the men in the Federal picket boats talking and singing. During this time we went out on an average of four nights a week, but on account of the weather, and considering the physical condition of the men to propel the boat back again, often, after going out six or seven miles, we would have to return. This we always found a task, and many times it taxed our utmost exertions to keep from drifting out to sea, daylight often breaking while we were yet in range....[1]

"If all went according to plan, and the weather had not forced them to beach the submarine somewhere along the coast, the crew of the *Hunley* probably returned to their dock at Battery Marshall sometime around 5 o'clock in the morning. As the submarine slowly maneuvered next to her slip, a weary William Alexander climbed out onto the cold iron hull and threw a line to one of the shivering sentries. While the ragged guards pulled the *Hunley* to her place at the dock, Dixon stood in the forward hatch, watching their progress. As the *Hunley* was once again tied up in her slip, a vaporous steam could be seen rising from the two open hatches. Dixon and Alexander slowly climbed out onto the dock and checked the ropes that would restrain their submarine until nightfall. As the exhausted crew men sluggishly emerged from the now relatively warm interior of the dark hull, their gaunt and flushed faces displayed the fatigue each had suffered from working the crankshaft throughout the night. As they gathered around the guard's small fire, talk of the recently ended patrol soon filled the frigid pre-dawn air."

"While the first hint of sunlight slowly started to appear on the Atlantic horizon, the weary crew of the *Hunley* dried their sweat-soaked jackets around the fire, and joked about the bad quality of the singing heard through the open hatch the night before. As a pot of hot coffee (or at least a reasonable substitute) was passed around the small circle, Alexander and Seaman Wicks unshipped the deadly torpedo and gently lifted it onto the dock. By now, the pre-dawn talking of the *Hunley's* crew would have been a common sound to the soldiers quartered near the Breach Inlet dock. As the first rays of sunlight appeared on the horizon, several soldiers wrapped in tattered blankets walked over to talk with the recently arrived crew. With the submarine once again gently rocking in her slip, and her crew now ready for the long hike back to Mount Pleasant, Dixon and Alexander lead their weary men down the beach past the numerous fortifications starting to stir for the day. As Dixon's weary crew walked by, the men of the various batteries waved their hats and shouted encouragement to the brave crew of the *Hunley* as they slowly moved past. When they reached their quarters, all flopped on their sandy blankets for a few hours sleep before they would once again rig the torpedo and return to sea."[2]

The above description is taken from Mark K. Ragan's outstanding book, *The Hunley: Submarines, Sacrifice, & Success in the Civil War.* Ragan has so graphically captured what it must have been like on these lonely and dangerous missions into the dark Atlantic that this author felt compelled, with his permission, to include it here. Only after reading the above can we begin to appreciate the tremendous difficulties, fatigue, and absolute terror that these men were willing to endure each night in the hopes of striking a blow at their enemies.

Because of the numerous near encounters with enemy picket boats, and the distinct possibility of not being able to reach Breach Inlet before sunrise, Dixon and Alexander thought it best to conduct an endurance test to see just how long they could remain submerged without surfacing for air. After the war, Alexander wrote in vivid detail about this unique and extremely dangerous experiment.

"This experience, also our desire to know, in case we struck a vessel (circumstances required our keeping below the surface), suggested that while in safe water we make the experiment to find out how long it was possible to stay under water without coming to the surface for air and not injure the crew."

"It was agreed to by all hands to sink and let the boat rest on the bottom, in the Back bay, off Battery Marshall, each man to make equal physical exertion in turning the propeller. It was also agreed that if anyone in the boat felt that if he must come to the surface for air, and he gave the word 'up,' we would at once bring the boat to the surface."

"It was usual, when practicing in the bay, that the banks would be lined with soldiers. One evening, after alternately diving and rising many times, Dixon and myself and several of the crew compared watches, noted the time and sank for the test. In twenty-five minutes after I had closed the after manhead and excluded the outer air the candle would not bum. Dixon forward and myself aft, turning on the propeller cranks as hard as we could. In comparing our individual experience afterwards, the experience of one was found to have been the experience of all. Each man had determined that he would not be the first to say 'up!' Not a word was said, except the occasional, 'How is it,' between Dixon and myself, until it was as the voice of one man, the word 'up' came from all nine. We started the pumps. Dixon's worked all right, but I soon realized that my pump was not throwing. From experience I guessed the cause of the failure, took off the cap of the pump, lifted the valve, and drew out some seaweed that had choked it."

"During the time it took to do this the boat was considerably by the stem. Thick darkness prevailed. All hands had already endured what they thought was the utmost limit. Some of the crew almost lost control of themselves. It was a terrible few minutes, 'better imagined than described.' We soon had the boat to the surface and the manhead opened. Fresh air! What an experience! Well, the sun was shining when we went down, the beach lined with soldiers. It was now quite dark, with one solitary soldier gazing on the spot where he had seen the boat before going down the last time. He did not see the boat until he saw me standing on the hatch combing, calling to him to stand by to take the line. A light was struck and the time taken. We had been on the bottom two hours and thirty-five minutes. The candle ceased to bum in twenty-five minutes after we went down, showing that we had remained under water two hours and ten minutes after the candle went out."

"The soldier informed us that we had been given up for lost, that a message had been sent to General Beauregard at Charleston that the torpedo boat had been lost that evening off Battery Marshall with all hands."

"We got back to our quarters at Mount Pleasant that night, went over early next morning to the city (Charleston), and reported to General Beauregard the facts of the affair. They were all glad to see us."[3]

During this period of intense training and operational sorties, Dixon was continually being asked by his company commander, Captain John Cothran, to return to the 21st Alabama in Mobile. Dixon and Captain Cothran were close friends, and on February 5, 1864, Dixon wrote a long letter to his old commander explaining his reasons for not returning. The letter, published in a 1900 edition of the *Mobile Register* under the heading, "Lieutenant Dixon's Last Letter," illustrates the young lieutenant's confidence and his devotion to the cause for which he was fighting.

"February 5th, 1864. Captain John F. Cothran. Captain Commanding Ceder Point, Company 'A' Twenty-first Alabama Regiment, Mobile, Alabama. Friend John: Your letter of the 29th came to hand today and contents duly noted. I am glad McCullough has gotten to be a Lieutenant, he has served long enough for it. You stated my presence was very much needed on your little island. I have no doubt it is, but when I will get there is far more than I am able to tell at present, for beyond a doubt I am fastened to Charleston and its approaches until I am able to blow up some of their Yankee ships. If I wanted to leave here I could not do it, and I doubt very much if an order from General Maury would have any effect towards bringing me back."

"I have been here over three months, have worked very hard, in fact I am working all the time. My headquarters are on Sullivan's Island, and a more uncomfortable place could not be found in the Confederacy. You spoke of being on the front and holding the post of honor. Now, John, make one trip to the besieged city of Charleston and your post of honor and all danger that threatens Mobile will fade away. For the last six weeks I have not been out of the range of the shells and often I am forced to go within very close proximity of the Yankee battery. I do not want you and all the company to think that because I am absent from them that mine is any pleasant duty or that I am absent from them because I believe there is any post of honor or fame where there is any danger, I think it must be at Charleston, for if you wish to see war every day and night, this is the place to see it."

"Charleston and its defenders will occupy the most conspicuous place in the history of the war, and it shall be as much glory as I shall wish if I can inscribe myself as one of its defenders. My duty here is more arduous than that of any officer of the 21st Alabama. Simply because I am not present to fulfill the duties of a Lieutenant, there are many that have formed the opinion that I am doing nothing. But I say that I have done more already than any the 21st Alabama, and I stand ready to prove my assertion by the best and highest military authority. What more I will do time alone will tell. My kindest regards to Charley and all enquiring (sic) friends. Hoping to hear from you soon. I remain your friend, George E. Dixon."[4]

Oddly enough, at the same time that Dixon was penning his letter to Captain Cothran, orders were being fashioned in Charleston that would have a demoralizing effect on the *Hunley* crew, but which, thankfully, spared the life of William Alexander who, after the war, wrote so descriptively of the submarine's operations.

"We were in readiness when I received an order which at the time was a blow to all my hopes, although only by obeying it did I live to write this narrative. On February 5, 1864, I received orders to report in Charleston to General Jordan, chief of staff, who gave me transportation and orders to report at Mobile, to build a breech loading, repeating gun (cannon). This was a terrible blow, both to Dixon and myself, after we had gone through so much together. General Jordan told Dixon he would get two men to take my place from the German artillery, but that I was wanted in Mobile."

"It was thought best not to tell the crew that I was to leave them. I left Charleston that night and reached Mobile in due course. I received from Dixon two notes shortly after reaching Mobile, one stating that the wind still held in the same quarter, and the other telling the regrets of the crew at my leaving and their feelings towards me; also that he expected to get men from the artillery to take my place. These notes, together with my passes are before me as I write. What mingled reminiscences they bring."[5]

According to Alexander, General Jordan had agreed to find two men as replacements. It is probable that one of the machinists, who had volunteered to accompany Dixon and Alexander to Charleston, was also ordered to Mobile on special duty, although Alexander fails to mention his name. Within a few days two men were selected: Corporal C. F. Carlson of Company A, South Carolina Light Artillery, and the other is thought to be a man by the name of Miller. It is also logical to believe that one of the Confederate seamen took Alexander's place at the aft ballast tank, and the two new members took their seats at the propeller shaft.

Within several days of Alexander's departure, the Union Navy inaugurated a bold new strategy which they hoped would put a stop to the speedy blockade runners which occasionally slipped into Charleston at night by hugging the shore line along Sullivan's Island. Soldiers on duty at Battery Marshall began to notice a swift sloop-of-war that would anchor each night near Rattlesnake Shoal, not more than three miles past the surf. She was the USS *Housatonic*, skippered by Captain Charles W. Pickering, who had orders to keep steam up and be ready to move at a moment's notice.

Dixon, too, had taken note of the Federal warship. If the fierce winter winds would subside, and the ocean swells moderate, it would take no more than a two-hour run for the *Hunley* and her veteran crew to reach her.

Union guns, elevated for maximum range, continue to pound the beautiful city of Charleston.

The Confederate water battery at Battery Marshall

A very poor quality map showing Breach Inlet and the back bays behind Sullivan's Island.

Courtesy of Mark K. Ragan

Confederate guns at Battery Marshall

National Archives

Chapter Eight
The Hunley Attacks!

The 1,240-ton, 207-foot, United States steam sloop-of-war *Housatonic* was one of four "Ossipee Class" wooden warships constructed by the Union Navy during the war. She was built at the Boston Navy Yard and had been commissioned on August 29, 1862. Immediately after her shakedown cruise, she was dispatched to the South Atlantic Blockading Squadron where she became part of the cordon of vessels blockading the port of Charleston. Commanded by Captain Charles W. Pickering, the *Housatonic* had participated in the many artillery bombardments that had ensued as the Federal fleet attempted to batter into submission the various Confederate forts guarding the sea approaches to the city. Armed with thirteen heavy guns, she and her tough crew were well prepared for any contingency by the time her anchor splashed into the cold Atlantic waters near Rattlesnake Shoal.[1]

During the first bitterly cold weeks of February 1864, Dixon and several of his crew gathered each afternoon on the sandy slopes of Battery Marshall to watch the enemy warship drop her evening anchor. She was approximately three miles out from the roaring surf, and by using a good telescope Dixon could make out every detail of the vessel in the fading light. Each night, however, the fierce winter wind howled over the ramparts of the earthen fortification, ripping and tearing her flag and driving all but the lone, shivering sentries to the heated bomb proofs below. Contemporary accounts indicate that the fierce winter weather during the first part of February severely hampered the *Hunley's* operations. During those frigid days Dixon, bundled in his heavy gray overcoat, could do little more than pace the beach, praying that the wind and sea would calm enough for them to make a run at the vessel at Rattlesnake Shoal.

With the Federal warship so near, and the probability that he could strike her before midnight, Dixon apparently modified his standard attack plan. All of the Confederate positions surrounding Charleston at the time utilized bright calcium lights, fitted with either a red or blue glass lens, to communicate with one another. The *Hunley's* commander arranged with the army officer in charge of Battery Marshall that upon a display of a blue light from the submarine, the battery would burn a white light as a homing beacon to guide them back to Breach Inlet. Evidence, to be introduced later, indicates that Dixon did indeed take one of these lamps with him on the fateful sortie.[2]

While Dixon waited impatiently for the severe winter weather to moderate, he wrote to his close friend, William Alexander, in Mobile. From his writings after the war, Alexander says that: "Soon after this I received a note from Lieutenant Dixon, saying that he succeeded in getting two volunteers from the German artillery, that for two days the wind had changed to fair, and he intended to try and get out that night."[3] This note, undoubtedly, was written on the afternoon of February 17, just hours before the *Hunley* set out on her historic mission.

During that Wednesday afternoon, Dixon and his crew were busy making last-minute adjustments to the *Hunley*. With only a moderate breeze now blowing out of the northwest, and a calming sea, all knew that tonight would be the night. Late in the afternoon, Dixon took them out in the Back Bay for one last run-through of their attack procedures and to check out the operations of the boat. From an article appearing in the September 1925, issue of the *Confederate Veteran*, more than sixty years after the event, there is confirmation of this from an ex-Confederate:

"Daniel W. McLaurin is perhaps the only man now living who ever set foot on the *Hunley*, the first successful submarine. During the war he served as Corporal and Sergeant of his company, and in 1864 he was on duty with his command on Sullivan's Island, near Charleston. The port was at the time blockaded by the Federal fleet, and the U.S.S. *Housatonic* was one of the blockading squadron. During the day of February 17, 1864, Corporal McLaurin and another member of his regiment went on board the *Hunley* to adjust some machinery, and of the incident connecting him with it, he says: 'As I recall, the torpedo was fastened to the end of an iron pipe, about two inches in diameter and twenty or twenty-five feet in length, which could be extended in front and withdrawn at ease by guides in the center of the boat to hold it in place.'"

"'Lieutenant Dixon landed and requested that two of my regiment, the 23rd South Carolina Volunteers, go aboard and help them to adjust the machinery, as it was not working satisfactorily. Another man and I went aboard and helped propel the boat for some time while the Lieutenant and others adjusted the machinery and the rods that held the torpedo and got them to working satisfactorily.'"[4]

With preparations completed and the day fading into twilight, Dixon and some of his men walked to the mouth of Breach Inlet where they were able to take one last compass reading on the Union warship. The ocean was relatively smooth compared to the previous few days, but because of the swells, Dixon knew that the enemy vessel would not be visible through the tiny glass viewing port until they were very close. It would be imperative, therefore, for him to maintain a consistent compass heading. Glancing skyward brought another concern to the *Hunley's* commander: the moon, which had just risen over the eastern horizon, would be very bright. If they surfaced a minute or two for air and confirmation of their course, they could be spotted easily by one of the enemy's steam-driven picket boats. A single blast from one of their howitzers could spell disaster. The bright night would also enable the *Housatonic's* lookouts to spot any underwater shadow or ripples left by the submarine as she closed on the warship. If Dixon and his crew were fortunate, however, perhaps a stray cloud would blot out the moon's light as they made their final run at the enemy. While his men conversed in hushed voices, the young lieutenant paced the beach, his eyes fixed upon the distant target. Concerned that the weather might again deteriorate, Dixon, in spite of the bright moonlight, felt they had waited long enough. The attack was on.

As the sun slowly slipped behind the distant church spires of Charleston, Captain Pickering was preparing his ship for another monotonous night of guarding the waters between Sullivan's Island and Rattlesnake Shoal. From testimony taken at a Federal Court of Inquiry held nine days after the attack, Pickering detailed his standing orders for the night of February 17:

"The orders to the Executive Officer and the Officer of the Deck were to keep a vigilant lookout, glasses in constant use; there were three glasses in use by the Officer of the Deck, Officer of the Forecastle and Quarter Master, and six lookouts besides; and the moment he saw anything suspicious to slip the chain, sound the gong, without waiting for orders, and send for me. To keep the engines reversed and ready for going astern, as I had on a previous occasion got my slip rope foul of the propeller by going ahead."

"I had the Pivot guns pivoted in broadside, the 100-pounder on the starboard side, and the eleven-inch gun on the Port side; the battery all cast loose and loaded, and a round of cartridges kept in the arm chest so that two broadsides could be fired before the reception of powder from the magazine. Two shells, two canister and two grape were kept by each gun. The Quarter Gunner was stationed by the match, with the gong. Watch and lookouts armed as at Quarters. Three rockets were kept in the stands ready for the necessary signal. Two men were stationed at the slip rope, and others at the chain stopper and shackle on the spar deck. The chain was prepared for slipping by reversing the shackle, bow aft instead of forward. The pin which confined the bolt removed, and a wooden pin substituted, and the shackle placed upon chain shoes for knocking the bolt out, so that all that was necessary to slip the chain was to strike the bolt with the sledge once, which broke the wooden pin, and drove the bolt across the deck, leaving the forward end of the chain clear of the shackle. I had all the necessary signals at hand, ready for an emergency. The order was to keep up 25 pounds steam at night always, and have everything ready for going astern instantly."[5]

As darkness spread its velvet mantle over Battery Marshall and the Back Bay behind Sullivan's Island, oil lamps were lit on the dock where the *Hunley* was moored. A few soldiers had gathered to watch the preparations, for they had gotten to know the men of the submarine and sensed that tonight might be the night. They watched as Dixon carefully checked the rigging to the deadly torpedo by the light of a lantern, while his men stomped their feet on the wooden dock in a vain effort to keep warm. Soon all was ready and the submarine's commander ordered his crew to begin boarding.

The little *Hunley* rocked gently from side to side as the men squeezed through the narrow hatchways and took their seats at the propeller shaft. While they were embarking, Dixon stood on the dock talking to Lieutenant Colonel O. M. Dantzler, commander of Battery Marshall. Two blue lights would be burned from the submarine when they wished to return, Dixon told the colonel. Nodding his understanding, Dantzler agreed that when the blue lights were observed, he would burn a white light near the mouth of Breach Inlet to serve as a homing beacon for the *Hunley*. With a final handclasp and a prayerful farewell, Dixon squeezed through the forward hatch and closed the cover.

Once inside, he lit the candle and placed it on the shelf as he had done so many times before. Turning to his crew he could not have helped but notice the grim determination on their upturned faces. They were veterans now, and would do anything that Dixon asked of them. Perhaps now more than ever he felt the heavy responsibility that rested upon his shoulders for the lives of these eight men. With a signal from

Dixon, the navy seaman at the rear hatch cast off the lines, stepped off the ladder, swung the heavy cover shut, and tightened the bolts. Dixon ordered the crew to rotate the crank at medium revolutions as he turned the wheel to guide the *Hunley* toward the mouth of Breach Inlet. As the boat slowly moved away, soldiers on the dock watched in silence as the submarine disappeared from the glow of the oil lamps. None realized that they were witnesses to a historic moment that within a few short hours would culminate in the first successful submarine attack in the history of mankind.

The actual events that took place that night on board the CSS *H. L. Hunley* can only be imagined. Staying on the surface until having cleared the shallow water and strong currents of Breach Inlet, Dixon probably took one last sighting on the three-mile distant *Housatonic*. Carefully noting the magnetic bearing, he would have begun letting water into the fore and aft ballast tanks until the small viewing port was awash. Ordering the crew to turn the crank "all ahead full," Dixon gently depressed the diving lever until the depth gauge displayed six feet beneath the surface, at which point he would have leveled off. It was now a matter of making slight course changes with the wheel in order to maintain the predetermined compass heading. Occasionally rising to the surface for a quick look and a small amount of fresh air, Dixon encouraged the crew to maintain the pace of the revolutions. If all went well, they would be there in less than two hours.

While we will never know the exact events that transpired inside the damp, dark walls of the Confederate submarine that bright moonlit night, we do know, according to the testimony given at the board of inquiry, almost every minute of activity on board the *Housatonic*. While the men of the *Hunley* spun her propeller shaft, driving her closer and closer, Officer of the Deck John Crosby stood on the bridge of the *Housatonic*, scanning the horizon for the telltale smoke or wake of a blockade runner. Lounging by the heavy guns, Federal sailors laughed and talked among themselves, while below decks, Captain Pickering was seated in his cabin at a writing desk updating a book of charts. Not far from the captain's cabin, Third Assistant Engineer James W. Holihan was carefully monitoring the steam gauges to ensure that twenty-five pounds of pressure was maintained.

More than an hour had passed since leaving Breach Inlet, and while the unsuspecting officers on the *Housatonic* went about their duties, Dixon decided it was time for another look. Raising the diving lever, he brought the submarine to where her two hatches just broke the surface. A quick glance through the viewing ports assured him that there were no enemy picket boats in sight. Several hundred yards dead ahead, closer than expected, were the twinkling lights of the *Housatonic*. Calling to the sailor at the rear hatch, he ordered the cover opened and within seconds, cool fresh air was flowing into the *Hunley*. After a few more minutes of running on the surface, Dixon ordered the rear hatch closed, and with a push of the diving lever, the submarine was once more beneath the waves.

Keeping his hand on the wheel and an eye on the swaying compass, Dixon probably turned to inform his men that after all of their hard work and training, they were about to strike a blow for their struggling country. With a cheer, the crew of the *Hunley* would have spun her iron propeller shaft with renewed vigor.

Unaware of the Confederate submarine that was now only a few hundred yards away, Crosby continued to pace the bridge while searching the horizon for the low silhouette of a blockade runner. Based upon his testimony, it is probable that the officer of the deck, unknowingly, saw the *Hunley* in the moonlight when she surfaced for air that last time. At the inquiry he stated that: "I took the deck at 8:00 p.m. on the night of February 17th. At about 8:45 p.m., I saw something on the water, which at first looked to me like a porpoise, coming to the surface to blow."[6]

Alexander believed that Crosby had indeed spotted the *Hunley*, for he later wrote: "Dixon, who had been waiting so long for a change of wind, took the risk of the moonlight and went out. The lookout on the ship saw him when he came to the surface for his final observation before striking her."[7] It seems clear from Alexander's writing that he considered the bright moonlit night to be the primary reason the *Hunley* was discovered while she was still some distance from the *Housatonic*.

"It was about 75 to 100 yards from us on our starboard beam," Crosby's testimony continued. "The ship heading northwest by west ½ west at the time, the wind two or three points on the starboard bow. At that moment I called the Quartermaster's attention to it asking him if he saw any thing; he looked at it through his glass, and said he saw nothing but a tide ripple on the water. Looking again within an instant I saw it was coming towards the ship very fast. I gave orders to beat to quarters, slip the chain, and back the engine, the orders being executed immediately."[8]

Rising carefully to where the glass view port just broke the surface, Dixon discovered the massive hull of the *Housatonic* less than a hundred yards away. Holding the diving lever steady with his right hand and gripping the wheel with his left, the *Hunley's* commander whispered to his men that they were almost there. Bracing themselves for the expected impact, the sailors of the *Hunley* spun the heavy crankshaft with all of their remaining strength, while Dixon, his face pressed to the forward view port, drove the submarine straight for the *Housatonic's* massive starboard side.

As the *Hunley* bore down on the *Housatonic*, Executive Officer F. J. Higginson rushed to the rail to see what had caused all the commotion. "It had the appearance of a plank sharp at both ends," he testified; "it was entirely on awash with the water, and there was a glimmer of light through the top of it, as though through a dead light." Unknowingly at the time, Higginson had actually seen the glow from the candle inside the rapidly approaching *Hunley*. At the same time that the executive officer noticed the glow in the submarine's forward view port, lookouts on the starboard side opened fire with muskets and revolvers.

With the sound of bullets ricocheting off the *Hunley's* iron hull, Dixon shouted for his men to spin the shaft with all of their might. Responding with a dedicated will, the interior of the submarine reverberated to the cheers of the Confederate sailors as they drove their submarine toward the side of the enemy ship.

At this moment, Captain Pickering of the *Housatonic* stepped on deck to find out why the crew had been called to quarters. "I sprang from the table under the impression that a blockade runner was about," he recorded. "On reaching the deck I gave the order to slip, and heard for the first time it was a torpedo, I think from the Officer of the Deck. I repeated the order to slip, and gave the order to go astern, and to open fire. I turned instantly, took my double barreled gun loaded with buck shot, from Mr. Muzzey, my aide and clerk, and jumped up on the horse block on the starboard quarter which the first Lieutenant had just left having fired a musket at the torpedo."[9]

A heavy thud resounded throughout the hull of the *Hunley*. Even though they had braced themselves as best they could, the men bowled over one another as the submarine slammed into the *Housatonic* at over six knots. With a splintering of wood, the serrated steel point of the torpedo buried itself deep into the timbers of the heavy Union warship. As the *Hunley's* crew struggled to regain their positions, Dixon shouted for them to reverse the propeller. Slowly the submarine began to back away. As the lanyard unwound from the spindle, the iron spar slipped out of its socket in the torpedo leaving the deadly device securely attached to the side of the *Housatonic*.

Referring to the boat itself, Pickering continued: "I hastily examined the torpedo; it was shaped like a large whale boat, about two feet, more or less, under water, its position was at right angles to the ship, bow on, and the bow within two or three feet of the ships side, about abreast of the mizzen mast, and I supposed it was then fixing the torpedo on. I saw two projections or knobs about one-third of the way from the bows. I fired at these, jumped down from the horse block, and ran to the port side of the Quarter Deck as far as the mizzen mast, singing out 'Go astern Faster.'"

"The men were huddling forward. I would not call them aft to the guns, as they could not be trained until the ship had got some distance from the torpedo, and they were in a safer place."

"I thought of going forward myself to get clear of the torpedo, but, reflecting that my proper station was aft, I remained there, and was blown into the air the next instant from where I stood on the port side abreast of the mizzenmast."[10]

Chaos reigned on board the *Housatonic* as frenzied Federal sailors continued to fire their revolvers at the indistinct shape in the water that was now backing away. Excited gun crews strived to train their heavy pieces on the object, while down below Engineer Holihan was desperately attempting to start the engines in order to move the ship astern. "I took charge of the watch in the engine room at 8 p.m....The orders were fully carried out on that night: to the best of my knowledge there was a little over 25 pounds of steam on, as we endeavored always to be rather over than under the mark. The fires were heavily banked and in good order....I was (in the engine room). I heard the gong beat for quarters, and gave orders to have everything ready for starting the engine. Immediately three bells were struck, and I gave orders to open the stop valves and back the engine. The engine had made about 10 revolutions, at the rate of about 30 per minute, before the explosion took place."[11]

Assistant Engineer Mayer also testified: "Three bells were struck a few seconds after I got there," he reported, "the engine was immediately backed, and had made three or four revolutions when I heard the explosion, accompanied by a sound of rushing water and crashing timbers and metal. Immediately the engine went with great velocity as if the propeller had broken off. I then throttled her down, but with little effect. I then jumped up the hatch, saw the ship was sinking and gave orders for all hands to go on deck."[12]

Seconds before the explosion, as the *Housatonic's* propeller began to turn in reverse, Ensign Charles Craven arrived on deck. "I heard the Officer of the Deck give the order 'Call all hands to Quarters.' I went on deck and saw something in the water on the starboard side of the ship, about 30 feet off, and the Captain and the Executive Officer were firing at it. I fired two shots at her with my revolver as she was standing towards the ship as soon as I saw her, and a third shot when she was almost under the counter, having to lean over the port to fire it."

"I then went to my division, which is the second, and consists of four broadside 32-pounder guns in the waist, and tried with the Captain of number six gun to train it on this object, as she was backing from the ship, and about 40 of 50 feet off then. I had nearly succeeded, and was almost about to pull the lock string when the explosion took place. I was jarred and thrown back on the topsail sheet bolts, which caused me to pull the lock string, and the hammer fell on the primer but without sufficient force to explode it. I replaced the primer and was trying to catch site of the object in order to train the gun again upon it, when I found the water was ankle deep on deck by the main mast. I then went and assisted in clearing away the second launch."[13]

Dixon and his men were stunned. The concussion from the exploding torpedo, only fifty or sixty feet away, must have been tremendous. The close proximity of the blast of ninety pounds of gunpowder may have loosened bolts and rivets or damaged the diving planes. Fortunately, the submarine was bow-on to the blast which would have somewhat minimized the effect. In the wake of the tremendous blast, Dixon struggled to maintain control of the submarine, while his crew gamely continued to rotate the crankshaft in reverse. It seems evident from Federal testimony at the court of inquiry that the torpedo exploded much sooner than Dixon and the crew of the *Hunley* had expected. This author believes there is a valid reason for this. The *Housatonic's* engineer, who was in charge of the watch, testified that the he had gotten the engine started and the propeller had made "about ten revolutions" before the explosion of the torpedo. While this would not have moved the vessel very far, with the *Hunley* backing away at right angles, it would have been just far enough to have pulled the lanyard across the bow of the submarine possibly causing it to jam in the spindle, thus pulling the trigger before the line had fully played out. In any event, with musket and revolver shots still slamming into the hatches and topside of the hull, and with possible damage to contend with, Dixon and his crew were now in a life and death struggle.

As the *Hunley* continued to back away, sailors below decks on the *Housatonic* clambered up ladders trying to stay ahead of the rapidly rising water. Sea water poured through the gaping hole blown by the exploding torpedo and with a sudden lurch, the Federal warship rolled violently to port. The *Housatonic* was settling rapidly by the stern, forcing her crew to scramble into the boats and rigging in order to avoid being pitched into the frigid waters of the Atlantic. Ensign Craven testified about these last terrifying minutes on board the dying Union warship:

"Feeling the water around my feet, I started forward and found the ship was sinking very rapidly aft. Almost immediately she gave a lurch to port and settled on the bottom. Afterwards in looking about aft—for the body of Mr. Hazeltine; I saw that the starboard side of the Quarter Deck, aft the mizzen mast—furniture of the Ward Room and cabin floating within, so that I supposed the whole starboard side of the ship aft the mizzen mast was blown off. I heard a report like the distant firing of a howitzer. The ship went down by the stern, and about three or four minutes after the stern was submerged, the whole ship was submerged."[14]

Another description is provided by Acting Master Joseph Congdon: "I drew my revolver, but before I could fire, the explosion took place. I immediately went forward and ordered the launches to be cleared away, supposing the captain and Executive Officer had both been killed by the explosion. The ship was sinking so rapidly, it seemed impossible to get the launches cleared away, so I drove the men up the rigging to save themselves."

"After I got into the rigging I saw two of the boats had been cleared away, and were picking up men who were overboard. As soon as I saw all were picked up, I sent one of the boats to the *Canandaigua* for assistance."[15]

Captain Joseph Green, commanding officer of the USS *Canandaigua*, recorded in his ship's log the concluding scenes to the sinking of the *Housatonic*: "February 17th, 1864. At 9:20 p.m. discovered a boat pulling towards us. Hailed her and found her to be from the *Housatonic*. She reported the *Housatonic* sunk by a torpedo. Immediately slipped our chain and started for the scene of danger, with the *Housatonic's* boat in tow. At same time sent up three rockets and burned Coston signals number 82 and soon after burned 82 again. At 9:30 p.m. picked up another boat from the *Housatonic* with Captain Pickering on board. At 9:35 arrived at the *Housatonic* and found her sunk. Lowered all boats, sent them alongside, and rescued the officers and crew, clinging to the rigging."[16]

In the aftermath of the explosion, 150 of the *Housatonic's* men scrambled to safety either in the boats or in the rigging where they were rescued by the *Canandaigua*. Five Union sailors were lost and presumed drowned. Meanwhile the crew of the "infernal machine" responsible for the sinking were endeavoring as best they could to return to their base at Breach Inlet. We cannot know what transpired within the iron hull of the *Hunley* after the successful sinking of the *Housatonic*, but the testimony of Federal Seaman Robert Flemming gives us a tantalizing glimpse: "When the *Canandaigua* got astern, and was lying athwart of the *Housatonic*, about four ship lengths off, while I was in the fore rigging, I saw a blue light on the water just ahead of the *Canandaigua*, and on the starboard quarter of the *Housatonic*."[17]

It could be that Seaman Flemming actually saw the prearranged signal from the *Hunley* to Battery Marshall, for as we shall see, a report filed shortly after from Colonel Dantzler stated that the signals from the *Hunley* were "observed and answered." As far as what transpired aboard the submarine that night, only one detail is known for certain: Lieutenant George E. Dixon and the crew of the Confederate States submarine CSS *H. L. Hunley* vanished without a trace, and were never heard from again.

The torpedo explodes against the side of USS *Housatonic*.

Naval Historical Center

The USS *Housatonic*

National Archives

A model of the USS *Housatonic*

Courtesy of Mark K. Ragan

Interior view of Fort Sumter, 1865

National Archives

A Confederate gun emplacement at Fort Moultrie

National Archives

Chapter Nine
The *Hunley* Is Missing

Sentries, pacing the ramparts of Battery Marshall that cold moonlit night in February, watched in vain for any sign that would indicate the return of the submarine boat. Over the long dreary weeks of January and into February, they had watched the *Hunley* practice in the Back Bay and had made friends with the sailors and army men of this new invention. As daylight broke over the eastern horizon, an ominous feeling of dread spread through the garrison. Something must have gone wrong.

As the day progressed the Union ironclads and occupied fortifications opened their usual artillery barrages while an occasional Confederate gun, striving to conserve ammunition, fired in reply. Those "in the know" on Sullivan's Island kept a vigilant eye on Breach Inlet, hoping that the black iron hull might yet appear. Because the torpedo's blast was well below the surface, there had been no fire or smoke, and very little noise. In fact, because of the haze, Confederate authorities were not even aware that one of the blockaders was missing. In addition, due to some mix-up by the officer of the day, it was not until Friday, February 19, that Colonel Dantzler was apprised that the *Hunley* was missing, at which time he filed this report:

HEADQUARTERS BATTERY MARSHALL,
Sullivan's Island, February 19, 1864.

Lieutenant: I have the honor to report that the torpedo boat stationed at this post went out on the night of the 17th instant (Wednesday) and has not yet returned. The signals agreed upon to be given in case the boat wished a light to be exposed at this post as a guide for its return were observed and answered. An earlier report would have been made of this matter, but the officer of the day for yesterday was under the impression that the boat had returned, and so informed me. As soon as I became apprised of the fact, I sent a telegram to Captain Nance, assistant adjutant-general, notifying him of it.
Very respectfully,

O. M. Dantzler
Lieutenant-Colonel

Lieutenant John A. Wilson
Acting Assistant Adjutant-General.[1]

This correspondence indicates that Dixon and his crew survived the blast from the torpedo and were preparing to return to their base at Battery Marshall. Evidently they had brought the submarine completely to the surface so that Dixon could open the forward hatch in order to burn the calcium light that had been carried on board. We can only wonder what transpired after he displayed the blue light. Did a sudden swell sweep over the *Hunley* and swamp her? Was she so badly damaged by the blast that even by working both ballast pumps the submarine could not be kept afloat? We know from Federal records that on her final approach the *Hunley* was met by a hail of rifle, shotgun, and pistol fire. Was the forward view port damaged or perhaps shattered by this fire?

Colonel Dantzler's report of the nineteenth arrived first at General Ripley's headquarters at Mount Pleasant, and shortly it was on its way to General Jordan of Beauregard's staff with the following summary:

"Head Quarters, Mount Pleasant, February 19, 1864. General: Lieut. Col. Dantzler, commanding at Battery Marshall, reports that on the night of the 17th, the Torpedo Boat went out from Breach Inlet and has not returned. The signals agreed upon in case she wished to return were observed and answered from that post. Unless she has gone to Charleston, the boat has probably been lost or captured. I have no reason to believe that the crew would have deserted to the enemy. They were not, however, under my directions, and I fear that it is more likely that she has gone down judging from past experience of the machine."[2]

The following day, February 20, appears to have been mostly free of haze, for from the ramparts of Battery Marshall, three masts could be seen protruding from beneath the water approximately three miles offshore. Several Federal tugs and barges were observed surrounding the sunken vessel, and it was quickly assumed that she had been the victim of the long overdue *Hunley*. Within hours the following report arrived at Beauregard's headquarters:

"Mount Pleasant, February 20th, 1864, Brig. General Jordan, Chief of Staff. Lt. Col. Dantzler reports a gunboat sunk off Battery Marshall, smoke stack and rigging visible, a tug boat and barge are around her, supposed to be the *Flambeau*. Another has not been seen since Wednesday night and it may be that she was blown up by the missing torpedo boat."[3]

After inspecting the condition of the sunken *Housatonic*, Captain Green of the Federal warship *Canandaigua*, filed a report that same afternoon:

"U. S. S. *Canandaigua*, February 20, 1864, Sir: I have examined the wreck of the *Housatonic* this morning and find her spar deck about 15 feet below the surface of the water. The after part of her spar deck appears to have been entirely blown off. Her guns, etc., on the spar deck, and probably a good many articles below deck, can, in my opinion, be recovered by the employment for the purpose of the derrick boat and divers."[4]

The news that the *Hunley* had sunk the *Housatonic* was received with elation in the streets of Charleston, but for some, who were aware of the failure of the submarine to return, there was little rejoicing. Still this brave act demonstrated that with ingenuity and courage, the Federal blockaders could be attacked and destroyed. Perhaps, now, other submarine torpedo boats could be designed and built.

An example of this glimmer of hope is illustrated by a letter penned by Augustine Smith, a sailor on the ironclad CSS *Palmetto State*, to his aunt a few days after the disappearance of the *Hunley*:

"Charleston, S. C. February 21st, 1864. My very dear Aunt Janey: The Yankees have not been shelling the city today, but occupied themselves occasionally with Sumter, but not often. Their guns must evidently be wearing out. For the last week or so all their shells have fallen short, and the other day of 100 thrown at the city, only 12 came in. The others fell into the water between this and Castle Pinckney. They do not seem to know it, or they would have stopped. A deserter who just came in says that both Gen. Gillmore and his men are heartily sick of shelling the city."

"The submarine torpedo boat, 'the fish,' which has been put in repair and been lying down at Sullivan's Island for some time, went out on Thursday night and it is supposed, sunk a blockader, as one of them was seen to go down. This attack was unknown at the time even at Headquarters. They supposed it was the storm. Since then, however, nothing has been heard of her and she is put down as lost. The common name given her is 'murdering machine.' The 'Davids' are ready for work, and I hope will soon be put at it."[5]

With the Charleston defenses under daily attack and the city itself under heavy bombardment, the news concerning the Confederate submarine soon became only a footnote in the stream of dispatches crossing General Beauregard's desk. He did, however, find time to send a telegram to Adjutant General Samuel Cooper in Richmond:

"To: General S. Cooper, Inspector-General, Confederate States Army, Richmond, Va. Charleston, S. C., February 21, 1864, General: A gunboat sunk off Battery Marshall. Supposed to have been done by Mobile torpedo boat under Lieutenant George E. Dixon, Company A. Twenty-first Alabama Volunteers, which went out for that purpose, and which I regret to say has not been heard of since. G. T. Beauregard."[6]

On February 29, 1864, the Charleston *Daily Courier* published a reasonably accurate story concerning the attack:

"On Friday night about half past 9 o'clock one of our naval picket boats, under command of Boatswain J. M. Smith, captured a Yankee picket boat off Fort Sumter containing one commissioned officer and five men. A large barge, which was in company with the captured boat, managed to escape. The officer taken prisoner is Midshipman William H. Kitching, acting master's mate of the United States blockading steamer *Nipsic*. The rest of the prisoners are landsmen."

"By the prisoners we learn that the blockader sunk by our torpedo boat on the night of the 17th instant was the United States steam sloop of war *Housatonic*, carrying 12 guns and a crew of 300 men. They state that the torpedo boat, cigar shape, was first seen approaching by the watch on board the *Housatonic*. The alarm was given, and immediately all hands beat to quarters. A rapid musketry fire was opened upon the boat, but without effect. Being unable to depress their guns, the order was given to slip the cable. In this the *Housatonic* backed some distance and came in collision with the cigar boat. The torpedo exploded almost immediately, carrying away the whole stern of the vessel. The steamer sank in three minutes' time, the officers and crew barely escaping to the rigging. Everything else on board, guns, stores, ammunition, etc., together with the small boats, went down with her. The explosion made no noise and the affair was not known among the fleet until daybreak, when the crew was discovered and released from their uneasy positions. They had remained there all night. Two officers and three men are reported missing and supposed to be drowned. The loss of the *Housatonic* caused great consternation in the fleet. All the wooden vessels are ordered to keep up steam and go out to sea every night, not being allowed to anchor inside. The picket boats have been doubled and the force in each boat increased."

"This glorious success of our little torpedo boat, under the command of Lieutenant Dixon, of Mobile, has raised the hopes of our people, and the most sanguine expectations are now entertained of our being able to raise the siege in a way little dreamed of by the enemy."[7]

While the sinking of the *Housatonic* did not cause a panic among the Federal blockading fleet, it was cause for severe alarm. Union sailors must have spent many sleepless nights after the sinking imagining that at any moment, with little warning, they too, could be blown out of the water. As a precaution against further such attacks, Rear Admiral John A. Dahlgren, commander of the South Atlantic Blockading Squadron, issued the following order to all vessels stationed off the harbor of Charleston:

"Flag-Steamer *Philadelphia*, Port Royal Harbor, S. C., February 19th, 1864. The *Housatonic* has just been torpedoed by a rebel 'David,' and sunk almost instantly. It was at night and water smooth. The success of this undertaking will, no doubt, lead to similar attempts along the whole line of the blockade."

"If vessels on the blockade are at anchor they are not safe, particularly in smooth water, without outriggers and hawsers stretched around with rope netting dropped into the water. Vessels on inside blockade had better take post outside at night and keep underway, until these preparations are completed."

"All the boats must be on the patrol when the vessel is not in movement. The commanders of vessels are required to use their utmost vigilance—nothing less will serve. I intend to recommend to the Navy Department the assignment of a large reward as prize money to crews of boats or vessels who shall capture, or beyond doubt destroy, one these torpedoes. Admiral Dahlgren."[8]

For a time, a rumor spread throughout the city (which may have been encouraged by Confederate military headquarters) that the *Hunley*, because of strong winds and currents, had gone into Georgetown (forty miles up the coast) after the attack and was safe. As time went on, however, it became plainly evident that the submarine and her brave crew were lost.

Alexander, writing after the war in the New Orleans *Picayune*, remembered when he first learned of the *Hunley's* success in sinking the *Housatonic*:

"Next came the news that on February 17th the submarine torpedo boat *Hunley* had sunk the United States sloop-of-war *Housatonic* outside the bar off Charleston, S. C. As I read, I cried out with disappointment that I was not there. Soon I noted that there was no mention of the whereabouts of the torpedo boat. I wired General Jordan daily for several days, but each time came the answer, 'No news of the torpedo boat.' After much thought, I concluded that Dixon had been unable to work his way back against wind and tide, and had been carried out to sea."[9]

By the end of February, little was being said in the press or official circles concerning the fate of Dixon and his men. With heavy shells continuing to rain upon the city and continued pressure from the ironclads offshore, there were more pressing concerns. Military officials who were well-versed with the details of the *Hunley's* operations knew that there was little possibility that Dixon or any of his men had survived. The prospect that the submarine had gone to another port or had been beached somewhere along the coast appeared hopeless.

Meanwhile, the Federal Court of Inquiry had concluded its sessions, and on March 7, 1864, published a summary of its findings:

"The testimony having been closed, the court was cleared for deliberation, and after maturely considering the evidence adduced, find the following facts established:"

"First. That the U.S.S. *Housatonic* was blown up and sunk by a rebel torpedo craft on the night of February 17 last, about 9 o'clock p.m., while lying at an anchor in 27 feet of water off Charleston S. C., bearing E.S.E, and distant from Fort Sumter about 5½ miles. The weather at the time of the occurrence was clear, the night bright and moonlight, wind moderate from the northward and westward, sea smooth and tide half ebb, the ship's head about W. N. W."

"Second. That between 8:45 and 9 o'clock p.m. on said night an object in the water was discovered almost simultaneously by the officer of the deck and the lookout stationed at the starboard cathead, on the starboard bow of the ship, about 75 or 100 yards distant, having the appearance of a log. That on further and closer observation it presented a suspicious appearance, moving apparently with a speed of 3 or 4 knots in the direction of the starboard quarter of the ship, exhibiting two protuberances above and making a slight ripple in the water."

"Third. That the strange object approached the ship with a rapidity precluding a gun of the battery being brought to bear upon it, and finally came in contact with the ship on her starboard quarter."

"Fourth. That about one and a half minutes after the first discovery of the strange object the crew were called to quarters, the cable slipped, and the engine backed."

"Fifth. That an explosion occurred about three minutes after the first discovery of the object, which blew up the after part of the ship, causing her to sink immediately after to the bottom, with her spar deck submerged."

"Sixth. That several shots from small arms were fired at the object while it was alongside or near the ship before the explosion occurred."

"Seventh. That the watch on deck, ship, and ship's battery were in all respects prepared for a sudden offensive or defensive movement;

that lookouts were properly stationed and vigilance observed, and that officers and crew promptly assembled at their quarters."

"Eighth. That order was preserved on board, and orders promptly obeyed by officers and crew up to the time of the sinking of the ship. In view of the above facts the court has to express the opinion that no further military proceedings are necessary. J. F. Green, Captain and President."[10]

In April, a letter addressed to General Maury arrived at Confederate military headquarters in Mobile. The communication was from Captain Gray of the Charleston Torpedo Service detailing what he believed to be the ultimate fate of the *H. L. Hunley.* Unfortunately, Captain Gray's analysis was faulty and incomplete, but his suppositions would be accepted as the likely fate of the submarine, and would be supported by historians for the next one hundred years.

"Charleston, S. C., April 29, 1864. General: In answer to a communication of yours, received through headquarters, relative to Lieutenant Dixon and crew, I beg leave to state that I was not informed as to the service in which Lieutenant Dixon was engaged or under what orders he was acting. I am informed that he requested Commodore Tucker to furnish him some men, which he did. Their names are as follows, Viz: Arnold Becker, C. Simkins, James A. Wicks, F. Collins, and...Ridgeway, all of the Navy, and Corporal C. F. Carlson, of Captain Wagner's company of artillery."

"The United States sloop of war *Housatonic* was attacked and destroyed on the night of the 17th of February. Since that time no information has been received of either the boat or crew. I am of the opinion that, the torpedoes being placed at the bow of the boat, she went into the hole made in the *Housatonic* by explosion of torpedoes and did not have sufficient power to back out, consequently sunk with her."

"I have the honor to be, General, very respectfully, your obedient servant, M. M. Grey, Captain in Charge of Torpedoes."[11]

While many accepted Gray's theory, there was still much speculation after the war as to just what might have happened to the *Hunley.* Until recently, most historians and researchers supported the theory that since the *Housatonic* reportedly backed her engines just prior to the impact, the *Hunley* was carried into the hole in the side of the Union vessel, caused by the explosion, and was unable to back out. Being trapped, the submarine was thus carried to the bottom with her. The fact that the torpedo boat, as it was called, had not been found near the wreck of the Union vessel, lent credence to this theory. A few researchers, however, including this author have always held a different view— a view which was proven correct in 1995. [12]

A detailed examination of the wreck of the *Housatonic* was made in November of 1864 by Lieutenant W. L. Churchill of the Federal Navy.

He had the ocean bottom dragged for a distance of 500 yards around the *Housatonic*. No trace of the *Hunley* was found. A salvage crew working several years after the war to clear the channel, however, claimed that they found the *Hunley*, and in their enthusiasm for notoriety, swore they saw bodies of the crew and turned the propeller. Several published histories concerning operations in and around Charleston have repeated this account. Most historians, however, have discounted this report because it would have been impossible to see anything inside the submarine at a depth of twenty-seven feet, and corrosion over the years would have prevented any movement of the propeller.

William Alexander, the man most responsible for passing on to future generations the history of the *Hunley*, also believed that the submarine had been carried into the hole blasted in the side of the *Housatonic*. In his opinion, contrary to design, the torpedo must have exploded on contact. Writing for the *Southern Historical Society Papers* in 1903, Alexander gave what most considered the final word on the fate of Dixon and his crew:

"The *Housatonic* was a new vessel on the station, and anchored closer in than the *Wabash* and others. On this night the wind had lulled, with but little sea on, and although it was moonlight, Dixon, who had been waiting so long for a change of wind, took the risk of the moonlight and went out. The lookout on the ship saw him when he came to the surface for his final observation before striking her. He, of course, not knowing that the ship had slipped her chain and was backing down upon him, then sank the boat a few feet, steered for the stern of the ship and struck. The momentum of the two vessels brought them together unexpectedly. The stern of the ship was blown off entirely. The momentum carried the torpedo boat into the wreck. Dixon and his men, unable to extricate themselves, sinking with it."[13]

In 1909, army engineers blasted the wreck of the *Housatonic*, because it was proving a menace to navigation into and out of Charleston harbor. Some speculated that the *Hunley* was mistaken as one of the ship's boilers and was blasted into oblivion. Recent research has uncovered a survey that was taken of the site before demolition, and divers reported finding several heavy guns and two boilers. The *Housatonic* had been built with only two boilers, and they were still in the wreck in 1909. Had the *Hunley* been present, and mistaken for one of these, the divers would have instead reported the presence of three boilers.[14]

It is unfortunate that many, including Alexander, did not have access to the findings of the Federal Court of Inquiry. These records were kept secret during the war, and in fact did not come to light until 1987. Those findings clearly proved that the *Hunley* was backing away at the time of the explosion. Also unknown at the time, was the report from both sides of the blue lights displayed by the submarine and the response displayed from Battery Marshall. While speculation as to her fate came and went over the years, all that was known for certain was that the CSS *H. L. Hunley* was out there somewhere—along with a brave army lieutenant from Alabama and eight equally brave navy crewmen. She had gone down in the nineteenth century, and it would be almost into the twenty-first century before human eyes would once again focus on her black iron hull.

This monument to the crews of the *Hunley* who gave their lives for the cause of the Confederacy is located in White Point Gardens at the tip of the Charleston peninsula.

Photo by the Author

Brigadier General Roswell S. Ripley, Confederate commander at Mount Pleasant
National Archives

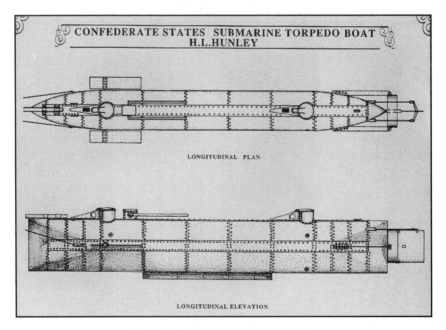

Plan view of the CSS *H. L. Hunley*
Author's Collection

Battery Marshall as seen from the beach

Chapter Ten
Discovery

As of this writing, the CSS *H. L. Hunley*, with Lieutenant Dixon and his eight crewmen, has rested on the bottom of the sea for one hundred and thirty-five years. During that time, many have claimed to have found her, but none, until recently, have presented evidence to substantiate their claims.

Shortly after the sinking, Federal divers visited the shattered remains of the *Housatonic* and reported that they saw no sign of the submarine. Several months later, the Union Navy dragged chains for 500 yards around the wreck hoping to snag the torpedo boat only to find a pile of rubbish. Not finding the boat lent credence to Captain Gary's analysis that the *Hunley* had been sucked into the hole blown by the torpedo, and that the Federal warship had settled on top of her. Alexander's writings after the war also supported this theory.

After the war there were many who maintained that they had found her. An example of one of these announcements appeared in the Charleston *Daily Republican* on October 8, 1870 under the banner: "The Remarkable Career of a Remarkable Craft." The author of this feature wrote that: "Within a few weeks past, divers in submarine armor (diving gear) have visited the wreck of the *Housatonic*, and they have found the little torpedo vessel lying by her huge victim."[1]

111

Another source reported that diver Angus Smith had seen the *Hunley* and that she was intact and resting on the bottom. Still other claims were made, some stating that they had even observed the bodies of the crew, but none of these claimants ever produced any evidence to prove their statements. Most historians are in agreement that these early reports were either exaggerations or purposely hoaxed. This was substantiated by Alexander himself, when speaking before the Iberville Historical Society in 1903, he stated: "I have been informed by Captain Charles W. Stewart, Superintendent of Naval War Records in Washington, that the many statements as to the discovery of the torpedo boat in the wreck are not authentic."[2]

In 1908, diver William Virden was awarded a contract by the Army Corps of Engineers to lower the wreck of the *Housatonic* as it had become a menace to vessels entering and leaving Charleston. After raising four tons of iron and blasting the remains of the Federal warship with dynamite, he collected his fee and reported that he saw no sign of the submarine.[3]

While it has nothing to do with finding the remains of the *Hunley*, it is interesting to note that at about this time, in the autumn of 1914 to be more precise, the British submarine *E-9* torpedoed and sank the German cruiser *Hela* while she was anchored near Wilhelmshaven in the North Sea. Thus the *E-9* became the second submarine to sink an enemy warship—just over fifty years after Dixon and the *Hunley* had ushered in the age of underwater warfare.

In November of 1970, Dr. E. Lee Spence, an internationally known archeologist and author, discovered a shelf in the sand three and one-half miles off Sullivan's Island which contained the partially exposed hull of what was thought to be the *Hunley*. Using sophisticated electronic equipment, Spence also found what was left of the dynamited *Housatonic*. In 1980, Spence filed papers in a Federal District Court claiming ownership of both vessels including salvage rights. While not disputing Spence's claim of discovery, the courts declined to grant ownership on grounds that both sites were outside of their jurisdiction. In fact, he was notified that if he continued to dive on the site without proper authority he could be fined and/or sent to prison.[4]

During the early summer of 1993, Mark K. Ragan, author, submarine expert, and diving enthusiast, organized a modest search for the *Hunley*. On June 10, Ragan and his team set out from Charleston harbor with the objective of pinpointing the remains of the *Housatonic*. Using coordinates supplied by Clive Cussler, underwater explorer and author who had conducted his own expeditions in 1980 and 1981, Ragan's team pinpointed the *Housatonic* by mid-afternoon. Using a magnetometer, it was determined that the remains of the Federal vessel were spread over a large area somewhat in the shape of a huge oval. After suiting up and diving on the area they found no trace of the warship protruding above the sandy bottom, which is not unexpected as the wreckage would have long ago buried itself several feet down in the soft ocean floor.

"On the following morning," Ragan wrote, "we returned to the docks to begin our search for the main target of our expedition—the final resting place of the lost Confederate submarine *H. L. Hunley.* By midmorning we had left the harbor far behind and were slowly approaching Breach Inlet, constantly monitoring the depth sounder so as not to run aground on one of the many hidden sandbars. Upon reaching the mouth of the narrow inlet, we anchored the ship and readied our magnetometer and underwater electronic gear for the search. Our plan was to take a loran generated course heading on the wreck site of the *Housatonic* that lay on the horizon, deploy the magnetometer, and steer for the wreck, while monitoring the sea floor with the bottom profiler."

"Within forty-five minutes after deploying the magnetometer, we got our first strike. We circled the area of the anomaly and found that metallic debris seemed to litter the ocean floor in all directions. After recording the location of the mysterious site with the loran, we came to the unsubstantiated conclusion that the wreckage we had found could very well have been that of the iron hull of a blockade runner that had run aground and been broken up and scattered by storms and hurricanes ever since. The conclusion that the wreckage we had found was that of a blockade runner was not that far-fetched, for within the general area of our search we knew of at least one other blockade runner wreck site. Although the wreckage we discovered was not shown on any chart, it was obvious that we had found the remains of some long lost vessel that had never made it to port."

"After the exhilaration of finding the supposed wreck site of a lost blockade runner had passed, we re-calibrated the magnetometer and continued on our course heading towards the wreck of the *Housatonic,* still over a mile and a half in front of our bow. Over the course of the next couple of hours, we discovered two more uncharted anomalies that caused the magnetometer's control panel to sound off sharply. The bottom profiler indicated that the large metallic objects beneath us were buried and did not protrude from the sand, while the depth sounder indicated that our finds lay beneath 22 feet and 26 feet of water."

"Within weeks after our moderately financed expedition was concluded, I had the paper on which we had recorded our loran coordinates notarized, so as to add some validity to our alleged discoveries. For the record our two greatest strikes were found at loran coordinates 45500.4/60489.9 and 45500.3/60489.4 between 10 and 11 a.m., June 11, 1993.

Although the signals given off by both of these two buried anomalies was very powerful, we had no way of determining whether either was the final resting place of Lt. Dixon and the crew of the *Hunley*."[5]

During the summer of 1994, Clive Cussler returned to the Charleston area, and in a joint venture with the South Carolina Institute of Archaeology and Anthropology, began an intense search for the submarine. The team searched almost fifty square miles off the harbor of Charleston in the first two weeks of August. During the last few days of the search, an anomaly matching the size and mass of the *Hunley* was found in the approaches to Maffitt's Channel. Mark Newell, archeologist for the state of South Carolina and leader of the team, reasoned that Dixon had signaled Battery Marshall from a location along a route from the wreck of the *Housatonic* to Charleston harbor's mouth where the strongest tidal flow would have expedited their escape. Instead of attempting to return to Breach Inlet, therefore, Dixon had decided that the speediest escape route lay through this channel.

In September 1994, a day was spent carefully probing and mapping the object with high resolution sonar. The team was able to determine that the target was within thirty to forty feet long, within five feet wide, and had a curved upper surface. Because of the approach of fall and winter, which would normally be accompanied by high winds and heavy seas, plans were laid for further exploration to take place the following summer.[6]

In May of 1995, Cussler's team, consisting of Ralph Wilbanks, Wes Hall, and Harry Pecorelli, and again in conjunction with the South Carolina Institute of Archaeology, resumed their search. Due to writing commitments, Cussler was not with the team, but was notified by Wilbanks as to how the discovery took place:

"The team's historic discovery had taken place on the afternoon of May 3, 1995," Cussler explained. "Ralph had tried to call me that evening, but I wasn't home. After hearing the wonderful news, I wandered around in a daze for three days before the significance of our achievement truly sank in."

"The find came one afternoon when Ralph had a hunch. After eliminating one of my grids, he decided to return to *the Housatonic* site and work farther east. After an hour, the magnetometer recorded a target that was appropriate for *Hunley's* metallic mass. Harry Pecorelli had accompanied Wes and Ralph that day, and he went down first to probe the target. Harry moved the silt until he touched a large iron object. He came up and notified Ralph and Wes that what little he saw didn't appear to be a sub, but he recommended further investigation."

"Wes Hall dove and enlarged the hole in the silt until it was about twenty-five inches wide by twenty-four inches deep. He identified what proved to be the knuckle on the hinge of a hatch cover. Returning to the surface, he announced, 'It's the *Hunley*. We've come down on one of the hatch covers.'"

"Ralph immediately swam down and enlarged the hole until the hatch tower was eighty percent uncovered. He noticed that one of the little quartz viewing ports was missing, so he eased his hand inside and discovered that the interior of the submarine was filled with silt, a factor that may well have preserved the remains of the crew."

"Satisfied that they had indeed found the *Hunley*, they returned to port, drove to the museum in Charleston, and stood gazing at the sub's replica. 'Do you realize,' said Ralph, 'that we're the only three people in the world that know what parts of the replica are incorrect?' Then they bought a bottle of champagne, went out to Magnolia Cemetery, and celebrated with the ghost of Horace Hunley."[7]

Many questions, however, still remain unanswered. Was the *Hunley* damaged by the gunfire it received from the *Housatonic*? Were there eight or nine crewmen aboard? Are their remains still on board, or did they manage to escape the boat only to be lost at sea? If they are still there, did any suffer injuries in the explosion of the torpedo or Federal gunfire? Are the hatches still bolted from the inside, or are they merely resting in a closed position? Are all of the keel ballast elements present, or was there an attempt to jettison the heavy iron bars? Are the sea cocks still shut, or were they purposely opened as Alexander reported that they had planned to do if they could not rise to the surface? Exactly how was the spar torpedo assembly rigged, and does any evidence of it remain? What is the identity of the third magnetic anomaly located during the 1996 National Park Service remote-sensing survey between the wrecks of the *Hunley* and the *Housatonic*? Could it be an element of the *Hunley's* keel ballast, or perhaps the *Housatonic's* slipped anchor? Based upon Assistant Engineer Mayer's testimony, the force of the detonation may have either disengaged or completely blown off the *Housatonic's* propeller. Could it be a portion of the *Housatonic's* drive train?

These are but a few of the mysteries that remain. Perhaps in the near future we may know some of the answers, for much has taken place since that day of discovery in May of 1995. Plans have been laid to raise the submarine, to provide a proper interment of the remains of the crew, and to hopefully preserve the CSS *H. L. Hunley* in the Charleston Museum where she can be seen for generations to come. As of this writing, those plans call for her to rise to the surface once more in the summer of 2001. (For additional information on the recovery of the *Hunley*, please see the appendices.)

It is only appropriate that William Alexander, the man who has taught us so much about the *Hunley*, should have the last word:

"When the historian shall in the future write the impartial history of the War Between the States, the South will then be seen in her true position and receive the justice and admiration due her for the many revolutions she accomplished during that trying period."

"It should always be remembered that when the war began it found the South, as she had been for many generations, an agricultural people, dependent almost entirely on the North to raise her food for both man and beast, to make all her shoes, hats and clothing, farming implements, and in fact, all and every kind of manufacturing article she needed—this because her lands and attention were all required to raise the staple to clothe the world."

"This was the situation when the federal government committed the first overt act and inaugurated war upon the South by attempting, with the *Star of the West*, to reinforce Fort Sumter and thus dominate South Carolina. Then almost before the South had time to look around her, she was hemmed in on land by Northern armies, and her sea ports blockaded by war vessels. But the necessity arose, and in a day she became a manufacturing people, supplying her needs not only with food and clothing, but also equipped her army and navy with guns, war vessels, and munitions of war manufactured by herself. Nor was this all, the South revolutionized the construction of the war vessels, of the world."

"From the article I have just read of the operations of the *Hunley*, it will be remembered that she rested on the bottom of Charleston harbor, the entire crew of eight men actively engaged, for two hours and thirty-five minutes before coming to the surface."

"They were the first, so far as history records, in all the world to demonstrate the possibility of successfully operating a submarine torpedo boat, years before much attention had been given to the subject. The *Hunley* accomplished the purpose for which a submarine torpedo boat was designed, vis., to operate underwater at sea, exploding a torpedo under and sinking the war vessel of an enemy in time of war. By this event the subject of successfully operating submarine torpedo boats received an impetus, moving the governments of every nation to make them important auxiliaries to their fleets. The plans of all the modern productions of submarine torpedo boats, when compared with the *Hunley*, are copied from the *Hunley*. Submarine navigation arrived with the *Hunley* forty years ago, and the *Hunley* was the product of Mobile, Alabama—a city in the South."[8]

Two views of the *Hunley* replica located in front of the Charleston Museum
Photos by the Author

Another view of the *Hunley* replica in front of the Charleston Museum
Photo by the Author

The battered Fort Sumter photographed from a sandbar at the end of the war
National Archives

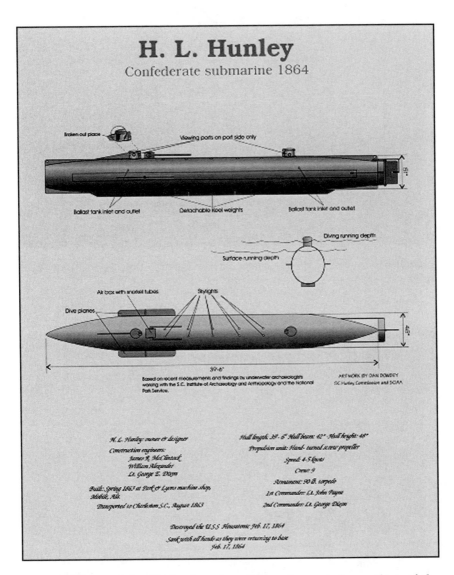

A plan drawing of the *Hunley* based on the most recent observations of the submerged hull of the submarine

Encrusted port side of the aft hatch. The view port *(center)* **and hatch cover hinge** *(left)* **are visible. Scale is one foot.**

Courtesy of the South Carolina *Hunley* Commission and the South Carolina
Institute of Archaeology and Anthropology, University of South Carolina

View of the forward hatch from three-fourths view of port side. The large jagged hole in the hatch tower may have contained one of the viewing ports.

Courtesy of the South Carolina *Hunley* Commission and the South Carolina
Institute of Archaeology and Anthropology, University of South Carolina

Appendix A

Crew members lost on board the CSS *H. L. Hunley*

August 29, 1863	Frank Doyle,	CSN
	John Kelly,	CSN
	Michael Cane,	CSN
	Nicholas Davis,	CSN
	(Unknown),	CSN

Lieutenant John Payne, CSN (Commanding), and Lieutenant Charles H. Hasker, CSN along with two other seaman escaped.

October 15, 1863	Horace L. Hunley,	Civilian, (Commanding)
	Thomas Parks,	Civilian
	Robert Brockbank,	CSN
	Joseph Patterson,	CSN
	Charles McHugh,	CSN
	John Marshall,	CSN
	Henry Beard,	CSN
	Charles Sprague,	Civilian

Appendix A

Crew members lost on board the CSS *H. L. Hunley*

February 17, 1864

Lt. George E. Dixon,	CSA (Commanding)
Cpl. C. F. Carlson,	CSA
James A. Wicks,	CSN
Arnold Becker,	CSN
Fred Collins,	CSN
C. F. Simpkins,	CSN
(———) Ridgeway,	CSN
(———) White	
(———) Miller	

Appendix B

(Press release on the discovery of the *Hunley*.)

NEWS

For Immediate Release 5/11/95

For More Information Contact: National Underwater And Marine Agency
Clive Cussler   1000 West Ave., Austin, Texas 78701

CHARLESTON, S. C.—Best-selling author Clive Cussler and his team of underwater searchers have discovered the legendary Confederate submarine *Hunley,* that along with its nine-man crew achieved everlasting fame as the first submarine in history to sink a warship.

Cussler and his team of searchers presented their findings, which includes still photos and video, in an 11 a.m. media announcement Thursday, May 11. The announcement was made within view of a replica of the famous submarine at the Charleston Museum in downtown Charleston, S. C.

Often called the Peripatetic Coffin, because it sank three times and killed all three crews, the *Hunley* sailed out of Charleston Harbor on the night of Feb. 17, 1864 and rammed her spar torpedo, packed with 100 pounds of black powder, into the stern of the Union frigate USS *Housatonic.* It then backed 120 feet away and triggered the charge with a rope. The explosion sank the Union warship within five minutes with a loss of five crewmen.

Though victorious, the *Hunley* failed to return to her dock and her disappearance has been a great source of mystery for more than 131 years.

The story of the submarine is one of tragedy and enigma. During her early experimental voyages, she killed her first two crews, including her designer and builder, Horace Hunley, who lies buried in the Magnolia Cemetery near Charleston. Final command was given to Lieutenant George Dixon, an officer of artillery, who blazed the trail in underwater tactics and launched the first school of submariners. It was Dixon who steered the *Hunley to* her rendezvous with destiny.

Numerous individuals and organizations have attempted to find the submarine's final resting place, but all failed. Beginning in 1980, Cussler mounted three expeditions that turned up nothing but finally achieved success on the fourth try.

Using a magnetometer, the search/dive team consisting of Ralph Wilbanks, Wes Hall and Harry Pecorelli struck an unknown metal target a considerable distance from the *Housatonic.* After diving into 20 feet of water and removing two feet of silt, they came upon one of the *Hunley's* two small conning towers.

"The sub is completely intact and remarkably well-preserved," said Wilbanks. "She can easily be raised using proper engineering and marine salvage technology."

"At first, we thought we only had a piece of old debris," said Hall. "But while groping through the silt, my hand came upon the hinges of the hatch cover."

Cooperating under a joint venture with the University of South Carolina, the search effort directed by Mark Newell, state archeologist, and funded by Cussler, dove on several buried objects with no success until luck led them over the remains of the famous submarine that P.T Barnum once offered $100,000 to anyone who found and raised it for his New York museum.

'This is without a doubt the greatest historical underwater find since the *Monitor was* located," said Cussler. "The difference is that while the *Monitor* is badly broken up and eroded, the *Hunley can* be raised intact and hopefully someday placed on display in a maritime museum."

According to the divers, the interior of the submarine is filled with silt that could very well preserve the bones of her gallant crew.

The *Hunley's* feat would not be repeated until August of 1918 when the British cruiser *H.M.S. Pathfinder* was torpedoed by the German submarine U-21, both ships also discovered in the North Sea by Cussler and his crew from the National Underwater & Marine Agency (NUMA) during the summer of 1987.

Cussler was especially elated over the *Hunley's* discovery since his perseverance finally paid off after some 15 years of searching.

"I wish I had a nickel for every time somebody told me I was wasting my time and that the sub wasn't out there, having been mistakenly salvaged along with the remains of the *Housatonic* several years after the Civil War," said Cussler.

Since NUMA is a non-profit foundation dedicated to preserving maritime heritage, Cussler states that the *Hunley* belongs to the people of the City of Charleston and the State of South Carolina, who he hopes will organize a campaign to raise and preserve her for future generations to examine.

The money for the years of search for the *Hunley* came from Cussler's book royalties. Referring to the hero in his twelve books, Cussler said, "Without Dirk Pitt, it wouldn't have been possible."

When asked how much he had spent on finding the *Hunley*, Cussler said, "Somewhere in the neighborhood of $130,000. But you know something, it was worth every penny."

Appendix C

Submarine Hunley found off coast, explorer says

By DAVID W. MacDOUGALL
Of The Post and Courier staff

The Confederate submarine Hunley, which sank in Charleston Harbor 131 years ago, has been found off Sullivan's Island, according to adventure novelist and undersea explorer Clive Cussler.

Cussler was expected to announce the Hunley's discovery today at a press conference outside the Charleston Museum on Meeting Street, where a model of the famous submarine is on display.

"There's absolutely no doubt," Cussler told The New York Times. "It's the Hunley."

Cussler, author of "Raise the Titanic" and "Inca Gold," has been searching for the Hunley since 1980 in a joint venture with the University of South Carolina. Cussler's book proceeds have been used to fund his underwater explorations. He set up a nonprofit foundation, the National Marine Underwater Agency, to search for famous shipwrecks.

Last week a team of divers found one of the Hunley's conning towers after digging through three feet of silt. The submarine is thought to be completely intact and covered with silt, Cussler spokesman Dean Foster said Wednesday.

The Hunley vanished Feb. 17, 1864, after it sank the Union frigate Housatonic by ramming it with a 12-foot spar to which a torpedo containing 90 pounds of black powder had been attached.

The Hunley was supposed to back off about 150 feet and trigger the torpedo with a rope. Instead, sailors on the Union warship said, the torpedo detonated when the Hunley was only 50 to 80 feet away. The blast is thought to have sunk both ships.

But the Hunley earned a place in history as the first submarine ever

See HUNLEY, Page 16-A

126

HUNLEY

from Page 1-A

to sink a warship. It was not until World War I that the feat was repeated.

In the last 131 years, numerous people and groups have tried to find the Hunley. P.T. Barnum once offered $100,000 for its discovery.

The Hunley sank twice before sinking on its final mission and all three nine-man crews were killed.

Cussler said he believes the last crew may be entombed in the Hunley, Foster said.

Cussler's divers knew where to look because they have been using a magnetometer to scan the ocean floor. The device locates large metal objects under the silt. The team scanned the bottom in the area where the Housatonic went down, Foster said.

The team made three dives after sweeping the bottom, and on their fourth major expedition, they found the Hunley.

Cussler plans to show underwater video and photographs at the press conference to back up his claim, Foster said.

Divers said the Hunley is well-preserved and raising it should not be too difficult, but Cussler doesn't plan to finance the salvage effort, Foster said.

The state of South Carolina and local governments will have to decide if they want to raise the Hunley and pay for its salvage.

Front page story in the May 11, 1995 edition of the Charleston *Post and Courier*

Courtesy of the *Post and Courier* and Mark K. Ragan

Appendix D

Updates from the University of South Carolina, Institute of Archaeology and Anthropology.

7/10/95

The contingency plan developed early last year for handling the *H. L. Hunley* is now in effect through the Hunley Project Working Group of SCIAA. It is the responsibility of this group to coordinate the technical expertise and methodology that will ensure that the vessel is accorded the very best protection presently available.

Two national scientific societies and five universities have been asked to advise the Hunley Project Working Group in the areas of underwater archaeology, conservation, and ocean engineering.

"The purpose is to ensure that all work on the CSS *H. L. Hunley* is conducted by the most informed team possible," said State Archaeologist and Institute Director Dr. Bruce E. Rippeteau. "It is important that the best advisors in our fields of expertise assist us in this historic undertaking. The Working Group has asked that the Advisory Council for Underwater Archaeology and the American Institute for Conservation of Historic and Artistic Works form blue ribbon panels to assist them in coordination and implementation of this research." The Hunley Project Working Group consists of three co-principal investigators.

Mr. Christopher Amer, Deputy State Archaeologist for Underwater has the responsibility of overseeing the underwater archaeology. Dr. Jonathan Leader, Deputy State Archaeologist and Conservator, will coordinate the conservation and stabilization of the vessel. The final co-principal investigator is Dr. William Still, noted author and Civil War Historian, who will oversee and coordinate historical research.

The South Carolina Legislature is establishing a State Commission to oversee the project. Details have yet to be finalized, but gubernatorial and legislative appointments are expected to comprise the commission's membership. The Legislature has also taken a strong leadership role in protecting the state's maritime heritage by increasing penalties for unauthorized disturbance of wreck sites that may contain burials and by seeking funds for the continued CSS *H. L. Hunley* research effort.

The University of South Carolina's University Educational Development Fund has already received donations for the CSS *H. L. Hunley* project from the public. The first check came from the Sons of Confederate Veterans Palmetto Sharpshooters Camp of Anderson, South Carolina.

9/26/95

The Governor of South Carolina has appointed a South Carolina Hunley Commission to oversee the disposition and scientific research of the *H. L. Hunley*. To date the National Underwater Marine Agency group have not released the coordinates of their find, which they are calling the Hunley. The SCIAA Hunley Project Working Group (HPWG) has prepared a draft proposal for the location and assessment of the site. This document presupposes that a precise set of site coordinates will not be available when the plan is implemented. The document is currently being reviewed by advisors from the Advisory Council for Underwater Archaeology and the American Institute for the Conservation of Historic and Artistic Works, the Naval Historical Center, and the SC Hunley Commission. The SCIAA HPWG would appreciate your comments on the proposal, which is included in two sections, below. Please include a brief statement of your professional expertise with your comments.

11/17/95

Through the diligent work of the SC Hunley Commission, several meetings have been held with the federal government and the Navy. These meetings are designed to define the nature and relationship of the cooperative fieldwork that will verify the vessel's identity and location, and assess its integrity. A programmatic agreement may be expected shortly.

The SCIAA Hunley Project Working Group (HPWG) has been pleased to assist the Commission in this work; and sees the discussions as an important step forward for this project.

Dr. William Dudley, Director of the Naval Historical Center, has reported to the HPWG that Mr. Clive Cussler has released the vessel's coordinates to the Navy. Mr. Cussler's action will most likely reduce the budgeted expenses for the initial phase of the project. The implementation of this phase is dependent on mutual consent of the Navy and the SC Hunley Commission and the cooperation of the weather. Results of the field work, when it occurs, will be reported as an update.

The *H. L. Hunley* is a war grave. The protection and appropriate treatment of the crew's remains, if and when they are encountered, has been an important concern of the HPWG, the SC Hunley Commission, and the Navy. Several members of the SC Hunley Commission have championed the public concerns and goals for the human remains. Needless to say, there has been a great deal of support for the careful and dignified treatment of the skeletal materials and personal effects. At the request of the SC Hunley Commission, the HPWG has prepared and delivered a statement concerning the scientific aspects of this issue.

1/16/96

The 29th Annual Meeting of the Society for Historical Archaeology Conference on Historical and Underwater Archaeology was held January 4-8, 1996 in Cincinnati, Ohio. An important session entitled Issues and Answers in Underwater: Civil War, Naval, and Western Rivers, was chaired by Robert Neyland and Dr. William Dudley of the Naval Historical Center.

In this session Mr. Ralph Wilbanks of the National Underwater Marine Agency (NUMA) presented a lecture on their search for the Hunley. The 35-minute lecture focused on the 1994/1995 attempts to locate the wreck site, and presented evidence of the finding by comparing archaeological and historical evidence. The talk was very well received.

While at the conference, SCIAA Hunley Project Working Group members, along with the Navy Historical Center, had an opportunity to view the entire underwater video footage of the site. The video image was viewed through a DOFI Raster Screen which enhanced, enlarged and sharpened the video images while adding to the depth of field. Evidence from the enhanced video along with the contents of the lecture, and the 1995 NUMA final report on the fieldwork, combines to present the best evidence yet for the site being that of the Hunley.

Meantime, negotiations are continuing between the South Carolina Hunley Commission, the federal government, and the Navy. When the negotiations are successfully concluded it is expected that a programmatic agreement will be signed by all the appropriate regulatory groups.

The Hunley Project Working Group continues to provide technical support to the Hunley Commission; and, to provide public information through lectures to interested groups. Technical comments submitted to the Hunley Project Working Group from this page and other sources are being collated and an answer page is in the works. Stay tuned.
Reference:

Hall, Wes and Ralph Wilbanks 1995 Search For The Confederate Submarine *H. L. Hunley* off Charleston Harbor, South Carolina. Final Report. Austin Texas: National Underwater and Marine Agency.

2/6/96

The SCIAA Hunley Project Working Group has assembled an updated *H. L. Hunley* Archaeology Management Plan. This plan replaces and incorporates draft versions which were originally posted on 9/26/95 and 11/17/95. Additional information about the Hunley is now available at the Civil War @ Charleston web page.

2/27/96

The South Carolina Hunley Commission met on Thursday, February 22, 1996 and reported major headway on the resolution of issues with the Department of the Navy. The South Carolina Institute of Archaeology and Anthropology Hunley Project Working Group was put on notice that the Commission hopes to be on the water within the next sixty days. This news was greeted enthusiastically by all present. We look forward to coordinating with the Navy Historical Center and the National Park Service Submerged Cultural Resource Unit on this historic undertaking.

The Commission invited the participation of Mr. Ralph Wilbanks and Mr. E. Lee Spence, both of Charleston, South Carolina; and Mr. Mark Newell of North Augusta, South Carolina. The South Carolina Department of Natural Resources (SCDNR) Division of Marine Resources has been requested by the Commission to provide an appropriate boat(s) as a stable platform for the additional equipment. The SCDNR has provided advice and assistance for the project since June of 1995. We look forward to working with all the professionals involved with the project.

4/8/96

The South Carolina Hunley Commission met on April 4, 1996, and approved a $33,000 budget request by the South Carolina Institute of Archaeology and Anthropology (SCIAA) towards the upcoming assessment of the Hunley site. The site assessment, planned for later this Spring, will be conducted by the National Park Service's Submerged Cultural Resource Unit, the Naval Historical Center, and SCIAA, with the assistance of the South Carolina Department of Natural Resources, Marine Resources Division. Additional specialized equipment and operator technicians are also being provided to the project on a pro bono basis by several companies and organizations. This equipment will be used to assess the integrity and condition of the hull, and will aid researchers in making recommendations to the Commission regarding future management of the site.

6/13/96

H. L. HUNLEY ASSESSMENT EXPEDITION FIELDWORK COMPLETED

Christopher F. Amer and Steven D. Smith South Carolina Institute of Archaeology and Anthropology.

The South Carolina Hunley Commission and the U.S. Navy/Naval Historical Center initiated on 29 April a jointly funded assessment survey of the remains of the submarine *H. L. Hunley*. The survey was conducted during a five-and-one-half-week period. The principal goals of this survey were to confirm the identity of the object at the site as the Hunley, document the site to the extent conditions would permit, ascertain condition of the hull, and to evaluate the feasibility of a future recovery project. The principal parties tasked to carry out this expedition were the National Park Service-Submerged Cultural Resource Unit (NPS-SCRU), South Carolina Institute of Archaeology and Anthropology-Underwater Archaeology Division (SCIAA), Naval Historical Center-Underwater Archaeology Program (NHC), and the South Carolina Department of Natural Resources (DNR).

Mr. Daniel Lenihan (NPS-SCRU) and Mr. Christopher Amer (SCIAA) were Co-Principal Investigators for the project and Mr. Larry Murphy (NPS-SCRU) was Field Director. The U.S. Coast Guard, the Naval Weapons Station, and Naval Criminal Investigative Service provided site security. A South Carolina Educational Television crew lived with the archaeology crew and documented all phases of the project. Several private companies and not-for-profit groups donated their unique expertise and an array of state of the art technology for remote sensing, geology, marine biology, sedimentology, and corrosion engineering. These groups include Marine Sonic Technology, Inc., Edgetech Corporation, Oceaneering Inc., Geometrics Inc., Sandia Research Associates, Inc., Jim Graham and Associates, and the Institute of Nautical Archaeology.

Phase One of the *H. L. Hunley* Expedition was carried out from 29 April through 6 May. This Phase consisted of non-invasive, remote sensing using a marine proton magnetometer, a RoxAnn bottom classification unit, a side-scan sonar, and a digital sub-bottom profiler. This sophisticated magnetic and acoustic sensing equipment relocated the site of the Hunley, defined the limits of this archaeological site, discovered other areas possibly associated with the site, and profiled the depth of the submarine below the sediments. Additionally, information from cores taken around the site provided environmental contextual information to assist in the assessment.

After several "down days" due to a series of weather fronts passing through the region Phase Two began on 9 May. This phase was designed to uncover and positively identify the *Hunley* by discovering and recording several of the hull attributes unique to the submarine. Attributes included the forward and aft hatches with portholes and cutwaters forward of the hatches, torpedo spar, diving planes, air box and snorkel, propeller, rudder, and external iron keel ballast. On 17 May, the identity of the *Hunley* was confirmed with the identification of five of the seven attributes unique to the vessel. While areas of the hull were exposed and being recorded, Mr. Dan Polly, a corrosion engineer from Jim Graham and Associates, conducted studies of the corrosion levels of the metal. Both phases were hindered by high winds and heavy seas.

Once Phase Two was completed the submarine was reburied under protective sediments. The site of this significant find is currently protected by physical barriers, electronic surveillance and sensing device to provide continuous security. The analysis of the data gathered during this expedition will take many months to evaluate. However, some preliminary results include the following: The Hunley is completely buried in the harbor sediments, lying 45 degrees on starboard side, bow facing the shore, dive planes elevated. The evidence suggests that, after the initial sinking, the hull became buried within 10 to 15 years in a single event. The hull still contains much metal, however there is active corrosion taking place throughout the vessel. There is little apparent damage to the hull in the areas investigated (less than one-quarter of the vessel). However, the forward face of forward hatch coaming is fractured, possibly where a port hole once existed.

Architecturally, the *Hunley* differs in a number of ways from a description and sketch produced by William Alexander some 40 years after the vessel was built, and is more in keeping with Conrad Wise Chapman's painting. The hull investigated has a hydrodynamic shape with smooth lines converging at bow and stern. The hull is 39 feet, 5 inches long, and approximately 3 feet, 10 inches in diameter. A 4-3/4-inch external keel runs along the bottom of the hull. Both hatches are present, each located approximately 9 feet from either end of the hull. Each hatch coaming contains a small view port on its port (left) side, while the forward hatch coaming apparently contained one facing forward but which is broken. The dimensions and configuration of the hatches approximate those noted by Alexander. A cutwater, formed from a single plate of iron, angles forward from the forward hatch toward the bow. The air box/snorkel is located directly aft of the forward hatch, although only stubs of the snorkel tubes remain. Between the air box and the aft hatch, evenly spaced along the hull, and to either side of the centerline, are 5 pairs of flat-glass deadlights, presumably to facilitate illumination of the interior of the vessel. The port dive plane, located below the air box is 6 feet, 10 inches long (longer than the 5 feet noted by Alexander), 8-1/2 inches wide, and pivoted on a 3-inch pivot pin. No evidence for a spar was found during the assessment.

When all of the studies have been completed a final report of the expedition and recommendations for the preservation and recovery of *H. L. Hunley* will be delivered to the South Carolina Hunley Commission and U.S. Navy.

8/8/96

The U.S. Navy and the South Carolina Hunley Commission signed a Programmatic Agreement on August 6, 1996 which spells out the respective roles of the state and federal government in the management of the Confederate Submarine *H. L. Hunley*. The agreement states that the United States will retain title to the *Hunley* while the state of South Carolina will have custody, in perpetuity. The Navy and the Commission agreed to cooperate on a number of issues regarding the vessels future treatment including site protection, archaeological investigation, conservation, and eventual display. A Hunley Oversight Committee was also established to guide the agencies in the management of the vessel. The agreement clears the way for South Carolina and the Navy to begin planning the archaeological excavation, raising, and conservation of the Hunley.

The formal signing ceremony in North Charleston, South Carolina included Senator Strom Thurmond, Chairman of the Hunley Commission Senator Glen McConnell, Dr. William Dudley of the Naval Historical Center, Christopher Amer of SCIAA, and a host of Commission members and other officials, all of whom spoke about the importance of the agreement and the remarkable cooperation between the state and federal government. In his remarks afterward Dr. Dudley stressed that it would cost several millions of dollars to do it right, but that it would be worth it. After the ceremony, Chris Amer and Jon Leader of SCIAA presented to the Commission the preliminary findings of the joint National Park Service-SCIAA Assessment Project which was conducted in May.

10/22/96

COMMISSION MOVES AHEAD IN FINDING HOME FOR *H. L. HUNLEY*

At last month's South Carolina Hunley Commission meeting, deputy state archaeologists Jonathan Leader and Christopher Amer briefed South Carolina Hunley Commission members on the results of the joint South Carolina Institute of Archaeology and Anthropology (SCIAA) National Park Service (NPS) assessment fieldwork conducted earlier this year. Commission members were told the position and orientation of the submarine on the seafloor, the analyses that had already occurred, the necessary work for the future, and that the submarine continues to corrode. Nonetheless, the hull contains metal and may be in good enough condition to be raised. With the full report on the fieldwork expected later this fall, Commission members agreed to solicit proposals from organizations that want to exhibit the submarine *H. L. Hunley*.

The Hunley Update is a Charleston's City's Best US WebSites Selection winner and has met with excellent response from the public. The South Carolina Institute of Archaeology and Anthropology thanks those persons who have complimented or otherwise expressed an interest in the homepage. Special appreciation extends to those individuals who have provided their thoughts on possible reasons for the submarine's loss on the evening of February 17, 1864.

1/8/97

The year 1997 begins with renewed resolve by the Naval Historical Center and the South Carolina Hunley Commission to move ahead with planning the future of *H. L. Hunley*. Deputy state archaeologists Jonathan Leader and Christopher Amer met in December 1996 with both groups to discuss criteria to ensure that the archaeological recovery, conservation, curation and exhibition of the submarine will meet acceptable professional standards in the field. A working draft of requirements pertaining to the siting and construction of a facility to conduct the work was delivered to the Commission and the Navy last month. We anticipate that a Request for Proposals will be announced later this year.

Research continues on the submarine. Scientists are still analyzing the data from the corrosion tests conducted on the hull of the *Hunley* but are optimistic that the hull can be recovered. The results of the joint South Carolina Institute of Archaeology and Anthropology (SCIAA)/ National Park Service (NPS) Naval Historical Center (NHC) 1996 assessment of the site will be presented at the Society for Historical Archaeology Conference on Historical and Underwater Archaeology in Corpus Christi, Texas on January 10, 1997 in a session on American

Naval Archaeology. Recent research involves the explosive charge and delivery system used on the vessel. No evidence of a spar was found during the assessment. However, an 1899 drawing by Simon Lake and drawings of Singer's Torpedo (drawing 1, drawing 2), of the type believed to have been used in the attack of the Housatonic, provide clues as to the appearance and possible configuration of the device, and a web discussion group is currently devoted to answering the question, "how was the torpedo attached to the *Hunley*"?

For the second time since its inception the Hunley Update has been presented an award. The Web Site Excellence-Anthropology award was presented by Wayne Neighbors, CEO of Vee Ring Ltd to SCIAA for its continued "excellence in public service" through the Hunley web site. In addition, the page is currently featured in Archaeology Magazine (January-February 1997) in the "Multimedia" section. Finally, the Discovery channel will be airing a special on the *Hunley* on January 19 at 10:00pm and 2:00am and on January 29 at 5:00pm. All times are EST.

3/5/97

STERNE AGEE TO SPONSOR HUNLEY FUNDRAISER

Alabama and South Carolina Unite in First Public Fundraising Effort for *H. L. Hunley.*

CHARLESTON, SC—Sterne, Agee and Leach, Inc., an Alabama-based investment firm with a branch office in Charleston, will sponsor "Raise the Hunley: An 1860s Gala." The gala is a formal theme party benefiting the South Carolina Hunley Commission's Save the Hunley fund. The event will be held on Saturday, April 26, 1997, at the Charleston Place Hotel in downtown Charleston.

The Raise the Hunley gala is the first public fundraising event sanctioned by The Hunley Commission. Mrs. Mary Wood Beasley, First Lady of South Carolina and wife of Governor David Beasley, will serve as Honorary Chairperson.

The Hunley gala will bring together philanthropists, corporate executives, academicians, and concerned citizens in a united effort to raise the *H. L. Hunley*. Invitations will be mailed to prospective individual and corporate donors by Monday, March 17, 1997. RSVP responses from invited guests must be mailed by Wednesday, April 16, 1997. Individual tickets are $150.00 per person, while corporate tables seating up to 10 persons are $1,500.00 each. Corporate sponsors are encouraged to contribute more than the cost of the table.

The event is black tie, with formal evening wear. The gala's menu will feature authentic 1860s Lowcountry cuisine, designed by Master Chef Frank Stitt of Highlands Bar and Grill in Birmingham, Alabama.

Speakers scheduled to date include author Clive Cussler, who financed the National Underwater and Marine Agency (NUMA) expedition that discovered the *Hunley* in May 1995; maritime historian Dr. Charles Peery of Charleston; Mark K. Ragan, author of "The Hunley: Submarines, Sacrifice and Success in The Civil War"; and South Carolina State Senator Glenn F. McConnell, Chairman of the South Carolina Hunley Commission.

Mrs. Mary Wood Beasley and Governor David Beasley are scheduled for statements as well. Charles Stuart, President, Stuart Communications of Concord, Massachusetts, is scheduled to coordinate the multi-media presentation for the speakers. Stuart Communications produced the Discovery Channel special, "Rebel Beneath The Waves", which telecast on January 19, 1997. Sterne Agee is currently arranging for additional speakers, which will be announced on this Web Site once travel arrangements are verified.

The gala event will also feature a five-foot scale model of the *H. L. Hunley* by master model builder William G. Thomas-Moore. Multimedia exhibits, depicting animation and videotape footage of the Hunley, will be designed by architect Glenn Keyes. John Brumgardt of the Charleston Museum will oversee all of the Hunley exhibits, which will show never-before-seen photos and depictions of the *H. L. Hunley*.

An auction will be held after the speakers' portion of the program, which is scheduled to include original artworks from nationally renowned maritime artists William R. McGrath of Cleveland, Ohio, and Randall McKissick of Columbia, South Carolina. A list of all auction items, and opening prices, will be posted later.

A dance will conclude the gala event, with an open bar. A five-piece 1860s theme band, provided by Events and Entertainment of Charleston, will perform. South Carolina's Civil War reenactment community is also expected to play a key role in the event's success.

At this time, the event is invitation only. Additional invitations may be offered to interested parties after the sale of 350 tickets and a number of corporate tables. Mailing address for Raise the Hunley is Sterne Agee/Hunley, P.O. Box 20311, Charleston, SC 29413-0311. A Hunley Gala information line will be established by March 17, 1997, to handle any inquiries.

Sterne, Agee and Leach, Incorporated, is headquartered in Birmingham, Alabama. The company was founded in 1916, and services customer assets exceeding $3 billion in safekeeping accounts. Sterne Agee has nine offices throughout six Southeastern states. The company is a member of the New York Stock Exchange.

Future developments will be posted on the Hunley Update Page beginning on March 17, 1997.

4/13/97

PROGRAM FOR HUNLEY GALA ANNOUNCED

LIMITED TICKET SALES NOW AVAILABLE FOR PUBLIC

COLUMBIA, SC—Final plans for the April 26, 1997, "Raise the Hunley: An 1860s Gala" were announced today by the investment firm of Sterne, Agee and Leach, Inc. Underwritten by the investment firm of Sterne Agee, the Hunley gala is the first officially sanctioned fundraising event in South Carolina designed to raise funds for the recovery and preservation of the sunken Civil War submarine *H. L. Hunley*.

The Hunley gala will be held on Saturday, April 26, at The Charleston Place Hotel, 130 Market Street, in downtown Charleston. Tickets are $150.00 per person, and corporate tables seating up to 12 persons are available for $1,500.00 each. A limited number of tickets are now available to the general public, and information on reservations can be requested by dialing 1-888-971-1222 (toll-free nationwide), or 971-1222 (Charleston).

Deadline for reservations is Thursday, April 17, for individual guests, and Tuesday, April 22, for corporate tables. Interested parties are encouraged to leave a message on the Hunley hotline at the earliest convenience, due to the shortage of hotel rooms in downtown Charleston during the peak Spring tourist season.

First Lady Mary Wood Beasley, Honorary Chairperson for the Hunley gala, and Governor David Beasley will serve as co-hosts for the event. The gala is black tie. The keynote speaker will be best-selling author Clive Cussler, who financed the 1995 National Underwater and Marine Agency expedition which located the *Hunley* off Sullivan's Island, South Carolina. Television producer Charles Stuart will coordinate a presentation with maritime historian Dr. Charles Peery and Mark K. Ragan, author of "The *Hunley*: Submarines, Sacrifice and Success in the Civil War."

All of the gala speakers were featured on the January 19, 1997, Discovery Channel progam, "Rebel Beneath the Waves".

Multi-media exhibits, produced by Charleston architect Glenn Keyes, will depict never-before-seen animation, photos and video of the *H. L. Hunley*. A five-foot, museum quality model of the submarine, designed by William Thomas-Moore, will be displayed at the gala as well.

The gala's menu, featuring aristocratic 1860s Lowcountry cuisine, will be prepared by Chef Frank Stitt of Highland's Bar & Grill of Birmingham, Alabama. Chef Louis Osteen of Charleston will be assisting Stitt. Both Stitt and Osteen are widely regarded among the leading chefs in the United States.

After the speakers program, a silent auction will be held featuring the works of nationally-renowned maritime artist William R. McGrath of Cleveland, Ohio. McGrath will donate the original canvas paintings for "Charleston at Sunrise, 1863" and "*C.S.S. Hunley*" for the auction.

Critically acclaimed artist Randall McKissick of Columbia, South Carolina, has been commissioned by Sterne, Agee and Leach, Inc., to paint the first authentic portrait of the *H. L. Hunley* in history. McKissick's painting is based on the latest archeological data provided by the South Carolina Institute of Archaeology and Anthropology at the University of South Carolina.

Other items such as books, specialized gourmet dinners, and travel packages will be available at the auction. A dance will follow, with period music performed by a Civil War Era theme band.

South Carolina's Civil War re-enactment community is providing volunteers to the gala program, giving the event a 19th century ambiance.

An estimated $95,000.00 in artwork, professional services and other items have been donated for the Raise the Hunley gala program.

Sterne, Agee and Leach, Inc., opened an office in Mount Pleasant, South Carolina in April 1996. Founded in 1916, Sterne Agee has its headquarters in Birmingham, Alabama. The Company currently maintains offices in six Southeastern states.

A member of the New York Stock Exchange, Sterne Agee services customers assets in safekeeping accounts that exceed $3 billion in current market value.

11/20/97

"Moving forward on the *Hunley*" read the lead editorial in the November 3 edition of Charleston's *Post and Courier* newspaper. The South Carolina Hunley Commission met on October 30, 1997 in Charleston. The main item on the agenda was to establish an eleemosynary (not for profit) corporation called "Friends of the Hunley" that will oversee the raising of some $10 million to fund and endow the project. Plans at present are to raise, conserve, and curate/exhibit the submarine. The Commission also discussed various possible locations for a permanent home for the Hunley. Experts agree that the vessel, when raised, should not be subjected to excessive transportation that may damage the hull and its contents. To date, both the Patriot's Point Maritime Museum, located near Charleston, and the Charleston Museum have expressed interest in taking on the project. Once the Commission and U.S. Naval Historical Center agree on a site, the recommendation will be sent to the South Carolina General Assembly for final approval. Senator Glenn McConnell, Chairman of the Hunley Commission, anticipates a decision in the Legislature during the next session.

The Naval Historical Center, the South Carolina Institute of Archaeology and Anthropology, and the Hunley Commission are currently working on the scopes of work to set the standards and parameters of future work on the submarine. These documents cover the various stages of the project, and include the archaeology, lifting, and transport to a conservation facility, as well as requirements for the building of a conservation facility, excavation of the interior of the boat (remember, the *Hunley* appears to be filled with sand), conservation of the hull and contents, appropriate treatment of the remains of the crew, and exhibition and long-term curation of the boat. Requests for proposals will be published in the Federal Register and interested and qualified parties who desire to conduct work on the project may submit proposals.

Currently, the Commission anticipates raising the Hunley at the turn of the millennium. Many factors will come into play to determine when the raising will be undertaken, not the least of which is having the necessary funding available and a conservation facility built and operational prior to the hull being removed from its protected location.

The Institute has been working with a naval architect to anticipate necessary requirement to safely lift the hull without sustaining damage to either the structure or interior of the boat. Calculations of the combined weight of hull and contents, including the wet sand, range from approximately 21-25 long tons. The low number is based on a 1/4-inch hull plate thickness traditionally used in descriptions of the Hunley. The twenty-five ton figure takes into account a 5/8th-inch thickness of plate. After the Civil War, James McClintock wrote to captains in the Royal Navy in Halifax detailing the measurements and features of his three submarines, the *Pioneer*, *American Diver*, and the *H. L. Hunley*. Evidently McClintock's intent was to garner interest in his work from that quarter. In that letter McClintock states:

"I modeled her [*Hunley*], and built expressly for hand Power. This Boat was of an Eliptical (sic) shape, with modeled ends, and looked similar to Surf, or Whale Boats, placed one on top of the other. She was Built of Iron 5/8 inch thick, 40 feet long top and bottom, 42 inches wide in the middle, & 48 inches high, fitted with canks geared to her propeller, and turned by 8 persons inside of her. And although she was a beautiful model boat, and worked to perfection. Yet like her predecessors, the power was too uncertain to admit of her venturing far from shore. This boat was taken to Charleston, SC, and destroyed the sloop-of-war Housatonic. Myself nor the submarine's gallant commander, who lost his life in demonstrating, her ———, considered there was any danger in going out and destroying any vessel. But the danger was in having sufficient power to bring the boat back. I would here state I do not believe the submarine boat was lost in the operation of destroying the Housatonic, but was lost in a storm which occurred a few hours after. I am aware the Federals have made a diligent search for her, and have made three different reports of having found her. Yet no descriptions that I have ever read are correct. [brackets added] (ADM 1/ 6236, Public Records Office, British Admiralty, Surrey, England)

Note—A transcription of the complete text of McClintock's letter will appear in a later update.

3/20/98

The South Carolina Hunley Commission met on February 19, 1998. The Commission voted to accept a proposal by the Charleston Museum for it to serve as a permanent home for the *H. L. Hunley*. This will involve constructing a building to house, conserve, and display the submarine at the Museum. Final acceptance of the proposal is now in the hands of the South Carolina General Assembly.

The Commission has created a non-profit corporation, the Friends of the Hunley, to raise the funds necessary to raise, restore, and curate the boat. Mr. Warren Lasch, a prominent businessman in the Charleston area, has agreed to chair that corporation. In March, Dr. Robert Neyland from the Naval Historical Center, Dr. John Brumgardt and Mr. Hugh Lane, Jr. from the Charleston Museum, RADM William Schachte from the Commission, and Dr. Jonathan Leader and Mr. Christopher Amer from the South Carolina Institute of Archaeology and Anthropology, met with Mr. Lasch to discuss the funding of the Hunley Project. Leader and Amer presented cost estimates for the various phases of the project, and Mr. Lasch is in the process of developing a funding plan. Individuals wishing to donate to the Friends of the Hunley should make their checks payable to Fund To Save The Hunley, and send them to: P.O. Box 12444, Columbia, SC 29111.

6/26/98

H. L. HUNLEY FEATURED AT SEABROOK ISLAND SYMPOSIUM

Seabrook Island Symposium participants discuss an interpretive model of the submarine *H. L. Hunley*. Left to right are John Horton, Warren Lasch, Christopher Amer, and John Brumgardt. (SCIAA photo)

On June 6, 1998 the Seabrook Island Symposium Committee presented their 40th symposium entitled, "The Discovery and Recovery of the CSA *H. L. Hunley*." Featured speakers included Mr. Warren Lasch, Chairman of the South Carolina Hunley Commission's fundraising organization "Friends of the Hunley", Mr. Christopher Amer, SCIAA's Deputy State Archaeologist for Underwater, and Dr. John Brumgardt, Director of The Charleston Museum. Senator Glenn McConnell, who was scheduled to address the gathering, was unable to attend due to pressing commitments. Ms. Drucie Horton, Seabrook Island Symposium Committee member, kicked off the evening by discussing the *Hunley's* significance. Mr. Lasch presented a history of the development and operation of the *Hunley* and placed the submarine within an historical context of the Civil War and submarine development. Mr. Amer, co-principal investigator of the 1996 assessment project, presented an illustrated lecture detailing the results of that project, which was conducted by the Underwater Archaeology Division of SCIAA, the National Park Service's Submerged Cultural Resource Unit, and the Naval Historical Center. Dr. Brumgardt addressed the future of the *Hunley*, which included possible scenarios for conserving the iron-hulled boat and unveiled plans for a *Hunley* wing to be added to the museum. Following the presentations, Seabrook resident Mr. John Horton moderated an audience discussion period, which included numerous questions from the audience, many of whom are retired professionals.

Earlier this Spring, the South Carolina Hunley Commision announced its decision that The Charleston Museum would conserve, curate and display the ill-fated submarine. In response to this, Dr. John Brumgardt, Director of The Charleston Museum, Mr. Glenn Keyes, Architect, and Dr. Jonathan Leader traveled to Maryland in April to visit the new Jefferson Patterson Park and Museum Conservation Facility. Dr. Robert Neyland, Naval Historical Center, met the group at the airport and ferried them to the laboratory. Ms. Betty Seifert, Chief Conservator, then spent several hours leading the tour and gave a detailed explanation of the facility's planning and operation. The state of the art facility is very interesting and incorporates design elements that may have a direct bearing on the Charleston Museum Facility to be designed.

SCIAA staff Mr. Jim Spirek, Mr. Christopher Amer, Dr. Jonathan Leader and Mr. Steve Smith continue to provide public lectures on the *Hunley* to organizations like the Sons of Confederate Veterans, citizen groups like the Civitans and Rotary, and at professional conferences.

Appendix E

Author's Note:

Although the Confederate Congress authorized the presentation of Medals of Honor during the War Between the States, none were awarded because of the war-torn conditions prevailing at the time. In 1896 the Sons of Confederate Veterans was charged with the duty of identifying and awarding these medals for "uncommon valor and bravery involving risk of life above and beyond the call of duty in defense of his homeland and its noble ideals."

On March 25, 1991, the Sons of Confederate Veterans awarded each member of the *Hunley* crew the Medal of Honor of the Confederate States of America. The medals were accepted by Caldwell Delaney, Director Emeritus, the Museum of the City of Mobile, in Mobile, Alabama, where they are now on display.

Confederate Medal of Honor

CITATION

First Lieutenant George E. Dixon
Corporal C. E. Carlsen
Seaman Arnold Becker
Seaman E. Collins
Seaman Ridgeway
Seaman C. Simpkins
Seaman James A. Wicks

**Attack of the CSS *H. L. Hunley* on the USS *Housatonic*
Outside Charleston Harbor, South Carolina
17 February 1864**

"With full confidence in the *Hunley's* value as an attack submarine capable of breaking the enemy blockade, Lieutenant Dixon persuaded the commander-in-chief to rescind a directive banning further use of the vessel. Despite the tragic loss of two previous crews and the prevailing opinion that service aboard the *Hunley* courted death, Corporal C. E. Carlsen of the German Artillery and five seamen from the CSS *Indian Chief*—Becker, Collins, Ridgeway, Simpkins, and Wicks—volunteered for duty aboard the vessel. Under Lieutenant Dixon's exhaustive training, the crew became proficient in the submarine's operation yet found that protective measures by the enemy—night lights and chain booms—and the prevailing winds and bad weather thwarted their plans. Finally, abandoning the relative calm waters of Charleston Harbor for the hazards of the open sea, Dixon and his crew—under cover of night with nothing to guide them but ship lights and dead reckoning—surprised, attacked, and sank the USS *Housatonic* with an improvised torpedo as the warship lay anchored more than two miles off shore. Despite sending a signal notifying shore batteries of their return, the crew of the *Hunley* was never seen again. Their mysterious fate remains an ironic twist to their enduring triumph as the world's first submariners."

Appendix F

SOUTHERN HISTORICAL SOCIETY PAPERS—April, 1878.

Torpedo Service in the Harbor and Water Defenses of Charleston.

By General P. G. T. Beauregard.

On my return to Charleston in September, 1862, to assume command of the Department of South Carolina and Georgia, I found the defenses of those two States in a bad and incomplete condition, including defective location and arrangement of works, even at Charleston and Savannah. Several points—such as the mouths of the Stono and Edisto rivers, and the headwaters of Broad river at Port Royal—I found unprotected; though soon after the fall of Fort Sumter, in 1861, as I was about to be detached, I had designated them to be properly fortified. A recommendation had even been made by my immediate predecessor that the outer defenses of Charleston Harbor should be given up as untenable against the ironclads and monitors then known to be under construction at the North, and that the waterline of the immediate city of Charleston should be made the sole line of defense. This course, however, not having been authorized by the Richmond authorities, it was not attempted, except that the fortifications of Cole's Island—the key to the defense of the Stono river—was abandoned and the harbor in the mouth of the Stono left open to the enemy, who made

145

it their base of operations. Immediately on my arrival I inspected the defenses of Charleston and Savannah, and made a requisition on the War Department for additional troops and heavy guns deemed necessary; but neither could be furnished, owing, it was stated, to the pressing wants of the Confederacy at other points. Shortly afterward Florida was added to my command, but without any increase of troops or guns, except the few already in that State; and, later, several brigades were withdrawn from me, notwithstanding my protest, to reinforce the armies of Virginia and Tennessee.

As I have already said, I found at Charleston an exceedingly bad defensive condition against a determined attack. Excepting Fort Moultrie, on Sullivan's Island, the works and batteries covering Charleston Harbor, including Fort Sumter, were insufficiently armed and their barbette guns without the protection of heavy traverses. In all the harbor works there were only three 10-inch and a few 8-inch Columbiads, which had been left in Forts Sumter and Moultrie by Major Anderson, and about a dozen rifle guns—un-banded 32-pounders, made by the Confederates—which burst after a few discharges. There were, however, a number of good 42-pounders of the old pattern, which I afterward had rifled and banded. I found a continuous floating boom of large timbers bound together and interlined, stretching across from Fort Sumter to Fort Moultrie. But this was a fragile and unreliable barrier, as it offered too great a resistance to the strong current of the ebb and flood tide at full moon, especially after southeasterly gales, which backed up the waters in the bay and in the Ashley and Cooper rivers. It was exposed, therefore, at such periods, to be broken, particularly as the channel-bottom was hard and smooth, and the light anchors which held the boom in position were constantly dragging—a fact which made the breaking of the boom an easy matter under the strain of hostile steamers coming against it under full headway. For this reason the engineers had proposed the substitution of a rope obstruction, which would be free from tidal strain, but little had been done toward its preparation. I, therefore, soon after summing command, ordered its immediate completion, and, to give it protection and greater efficiency, directed that two lines of torpedoes be planted a few hundred yards in advance of it. But before the order could be carried out, a strong southerly storm broke the timber boom in several places, leaving the channel unprotected, except by the guns of Forts Sumter and Moultrie. Fortunately, however, the Federal fleet made no effort to enter the harbor, as it might have done if it had made the attempt at night. A few days later the rope obstruction and torpedoes were in position, and so remained without serious injury till the end of the war.

The rope obstruction was made of two heavy cables, about five or six feet apart, the one below the other, and connected together by a network of smaller ropes. The anchors were made fast to the lower cable, and the buoys or floats to the upper one. The upper cable carried a fringe of smaller ropes, about three-fourths of an inch in diameter by fifty feet long, which floated as so many "streamers" on the surface, destined to foul the screw propeller of any steamer which might attempt to pass over the obstruction. Shortly after these cables were in position a blockade-runner, in attempting at night to pass through the gap purposely left open near the Sullivan Island shore, under the guns of Fort Moultrie and of the outside batteries, accidentally crossed the end of the rope obstruction, when one of the streamers got entangled around the shaft, checking its revolutions. The vessel was at once compelled to drop anchor to avoid drifting on the torpedoes or ashore, and afterward had to be docked for the removal of the streamer before she could again use her propeller. The torpedoes, as anchored, floated a few feet below the surface of the water at low tide, and were loaded with one hundred pounds of powder arranged to explode by concussion—the automatic fuse employed being the invention of Capt. Francis D. Lee, an intelligent young engineer officer of my general staff, and now a prominent architect in St. Louis. The fuse or firing apparatus consisted of a cylindrical lead tube with a hemispherical head, the metal in the head being thinner than at the sides. The tube was open at the lower extremity, where it was surrounded by a flange; and, when in place, it was protected against leakage by means of brass couplings and rubber washers. It was charged as follows: In its center was a glass tube filled with sulfuric acid and hermetically sealed. This was guarded by another glass tube sealed in like manner, and both were retained in position by means of a peculiar pin at the open end of the leaden tube; the space between the latter and the glass tube was then filled with a composition of chlorate of potassa and powdered loaf sugar, with a quantity of rifle powder. The lower part of the tube was then closed with a piece of oiled paper. Great care had to be taken to ascertain that the leaden tube was perfectly water-tight under considerable pressure. The torpedo also had to undergo the most careful test. The firing of the tube was produced by bringing the thin head in contact with a hard object, as the side of a vessel; the indentation of the lead broke the glass tubes, which discharged the acid on the composition, firing it, and thereby igniting the charge in the torpedo.

The charges used varied from sixty to one hundred pounds rifle powder, though other explosives might have been more advantageously used if they had been available to us. Generally four of the fuses were attached to the head of each torpedo so as to secure the discharge at any angle of attack. These firing tubes or fuses were afterward modified to avoid the great risk consequent upon screwing them in place and of having them permanently attached to the charged torpedo. The shell of the latter was thinned at the point where the tube was attached, so that, under water pressure, the explosion of the tube would certainly break it and discharge the torpedo; though, when unsubmerged, the explosion of the tube would vent itself in the open air without breaking the shell. In this arrangement the tube was of brass, with a leaden head, and made water-tight by means of a screw plug at its base. Both the shell and the tube being made independently water-tight, the screw connection between the two was made loose, so that the tube could be attached or detached readily with the fingers. The mode adopted for testing against leakage was by placing them in a vessel of alcohol, under the glass exhaust of an air-pump. When no air bubbles appeared the tubes could be relied on. Captain Lee had also an electric torpedo which exploded by concussion against a hard object; the electric current being thus established, insured the discharge at the right moment.

Captain Lee is the inventor also of the "spar-torpedo" as an attachment to vessels, now in general use in the Federal navy. It originated as follows: He reported to me that he thought he could blow up successfully any vessel by means of a torpedo carried some five or six feet under water at the end of a pole ten or twelve feet long, which should be attached to the bow of a skiff or row-boat. I authorized an experiment upon the hulk of an unfinished and condemned gunboat anchored in the harbor, and loaded for the purpose with all kinds of rubbish taken from the "burnt district" of the city. It was a complete success; a large hole was made in the side of the hulk, the rubbish being blow high in the air, and the vessel sank in less than a minute. I then determined to employ this important invention, not only in the defense of Charleston, but to disperse or destroy the Federal blockading fleet by means of one or more small swift steamers, with low decks, and armed only with "spar-torpedoes" as designed by Captain Lee. I sent him at once to Richmond, to urge the matter on the attention of the Confederate Government. He reported his mission as follows:

"In compliance with your orders, I submitted the drawing of my torpedo and a vessel with which I propose to operate them, to the Secretary of War. While he heartily approved, he stated his inability to act in the matter, as it was a subject that appertained to the navy. He, however, introduced me and urged it to the Secretary of Navy. The Secretary of War could do nothing, and the Secretary of the Navy would not, for the reason that I was not a naval officer under his command. So I returned to Charleston without accomplishing anything. After a lapse of some months I was again sent to Richmond to represent the matter to the Government, and I carried with me the endorsement of the best officers of the navy. The result was the transfer of an unfinished hull, on the stocks at Charleston, which was designed for a gunboat—or rather floating battery, as she was not arranged for any motive power, but was intended to be anchored in position. This hull was completed by me, and a second-hand and much worn engine was obtained in Savannah and placed in her. Notwithstanding her tub-like model and the inefficiency of her engine, Captain Carlin, commanding a blockade-runner, took charge of her in an attack against the *New Ironsides*. She was furnished with a spar designed to carry three torpedoes of one hundred pounds each. The lateral spars suggested by you, Captain Carlin declined to use, as they would interfere very seriously with the movements of the vessel, which, even without them, could with the utmost difficulty stem the current. The boat was almost entirely submerged, and painted gray like the blockade runners, and, like them, made no smoke, by burning anthracite coal. The night selected for the attack was very dark, and the *New Ironsides* was not seen until quite near. Captain Carlin immediately made for her; but her side being oblique to the direction of his approach, he ordered his steersman, who was below deck, to change the course. This order was misunderstood, and, in place of going the 'bow on' as was proposed, she ran alongside of the *New Ironsides* and entangled her spar in the anchor-chain of that vessel. In attempting to back the engine hung on the center, and some delay occurred before it was pried off. During this critical period Captain Carlin, in answer to threats and inquiries, declared his boat to be the *Live Yankee*, from Port Royal, with dispatches for the admiral. This deception was not discovered until after Carlin had backed out and his vessel was lost in the darkness."

Shortly after this bold attempt of Captain Carlin, in the summer of 1863, to blow up the *New Ironsides*, Mr. Theodore Stone, Dr. Ravenel, and other gentlemen of Charleston, had built a small cigar-shaped boat, which they called the *David*. It had been specially planned and constructed to attack this much-dreaded naval Goliath, the *New Ironsides*. It was about twenty feet long, with a diameter of five feet at its middle, and was propelled by a small screw worked by a diminutive engine. As soon as ready for service, I caused it to be fitted with a "Lee spar-torpedo" charged with seventy-five pounds of powder. Commander W. T. Glassel, a brave and enterprising officer of the Confederate States Navy, took charge of it, and about eight o'clock one hazy night, on the ebb tide, with a crew of one engineer, J. H. Tomb; one fireman, James Sullivan; and a pilot, J. W. Cannon; he fearlessly set forth from Charleston on his perilous mission—the destruction of the *New Ironsides*. I may note that this ironclad steamer threw a great deal more metal, at each broadside, than all the monitors together of the fleet; her fire was delivered with more rapidity and accuracy, and she was the most effective vessel employed in the reduction of Battery Wagner.

The *David* reached the *New Ironsides* about ten o'clock p.m., striking her with a torpedo about six feet under water, but fortunately for that steamer she received the shock against one of her inner bulk-heads, which saved her from destruction. The water, however, being thrown up in large volume, half-filled her little assailant and extinguished its fires. It then drifted out to sea with the current, under a heavy grape and musketry fire from the much alarmed crew of the *New Ironsides*. Supposing the *David* disabled, Glassel and his men jumped into the sea to swim ashore; but after remaining in the water about one hour he was picked up by the boat of a Federal transport schooner, whence he was transferred to the guard ship *Ottowa*, lying outside of the rest of the fleet. He was ordered at first, by Admiral Dahlgren, to be ironed, and in case of resistance, to be double ironed; but through the intercession of his friend, Captain W. D. Whiting, commanding the *Ottawa*, he was released on giving his parole not to attempt to escape from the ship. The fireman, Sullivan, had taken refuge on the rudder of the *New Ironsides*, where he was discovered, put in irons and kept in a dark cell until sent with Glassel to New York, to be tried and hung, as reported by Northern newspapers, for using an engine of war not recognized by civilized nations. But the government of the United States has now a torpedo corps, intended specially to study and develop that important branch of the military service. After a captivity of many months in Forts Lafayette and Warren, Glassel and Sullivan were finally exchanged for the captain and a sailor of the Federal steamer *Isaac Smith*, a heavily-armed gunboat which was captured in the Stono river, with its entire crew of one hundred and thirty officers and men, by a surprise I had prepared, with field artillery only, placed in ambuscade along the river bank, and under whose fire the Federal gunners were unable to man and use their powerful guns. Captain Glassel's other two companions, Engineer Tomb and Pilot Cannon, after swimming about for a while, espied the *David* still afloat, drifting with the current; they betook themselves to it, re-lit the fires from its bull's-eye lantern, got up steam and started back for the city; they had to re-pass through the fleet and they received the fire of several of its monitors and guard-boats, fortunately without injury. With the assistance of the flood tide they returned to their point of departure, at the Atlantic wharf, about midnight, after having performed one of the most daring feats of the war. The *New Ironsides* never fired another shot after this attack upon her. She remained some time at her anchorage off Morris Island, evidently undergoing repairs; she was then towed to Port Royal, probably to fit her for her voyage to Philadelphia, where she remained until destroyed by fire after the war.

Nearly about the time of the attack upon the *New Ironsides* by the *David*, Mr. Horace L. Hunley, formerly of New Orleans, but then living in Mobile, offered me another torpedo-boat of a different description, which had been built with his private means. It was shaped like a fish, made of galvanized iron, was twenty feet long, and at the middle three and a half feet wide by five deep. From its shape it came to be known as the "fish torpedo-boat." Propelled by a screw worked from the inside by seven or eight men, it was so contrived that it could be submerged and worked under water for several hours, and to this end was provided with a fin on each side, worked also from the interior. By depressing the points of these fins the boat, when in motion, was made to descend, and by elevating them it was made to rise. Light was afforded through the means of bull's-eyes placed in the man-holes. Lieut. Payne, Confederate States Navy, having volunteered with a crew from the Confederacy Navy, to man the fish-boat for another attack upon the *New Ironsides*, it was given into their hands for that purpose. While tied to the wharf at Fort Johnston, whence it was to start under cover of night to make the attack, a steamer passing close by capsized and sunk it. Lieut. Payne, who at the time was standing in one of the man-holes, jumped out into the water, which, rushing into the two openings, drowned two men then within the body of the boat. After the recovery of the sunken boat Mr. Hunley came from Mobile, bringing with him Lieutenant Dixon, of the Alabama Volunteers, who had successfully experimented with the boat in the harbor of Mobile, and under him another naval crew volunteered to work it. As originally designed, the torpedo was to be dragged astern upon the surface of the water; the boat, approaching the broadside of the vessel to be attacked, was to dive beneath it, and, rising to the surface beyond, continue its course, thus bringing the floating torpedo against the vessel's side, when it would be discharged by a trigger contrived to go off by the contact. Lieutenant Dixon made repeated descents in the harbor of Charleston, diving under the naval receiving ship which lay at anchor there. But one day when he was absent from the city Mr. Hunley, unfortunately, wishing to handle the boat himself, made the attempt. It was readily submerged, but did not rise again to the surface, and all on board perished from asphyxiation. When the boat was discovered, raised and opened, the spectacle was indescribably ghastly; the unfortunate men were contorted into all kinds of horrible attitudes; some clutching candles, evidently endeavoring to force open the man-holes; others lying in the bottom tightly grappled together, and the blackened faces of all presented the expression of their despair and agony. After this tragedy I refused to permit the boat to be used again; but Lieutenant Dixon, a brave and determined man, having returned to Charleston, applied to me for authority to use it against the Federal steam sloop-of-war *Housatonic*, a powerful new vessel, carrying eleven guns of the largest caliber, which lay at the time in the north channel opposite Beach Inlet, materially obstructing the passage of our blockade-runners in and out. At the suggestion of my chief-of-staff, Gen. Jordan,

I consented to its use for this purpose, not as a submarine machine, but in the same manner as the *David*. As the *Housatonic* was easily approached through interior channels from behind Sullivan's Island, and Lieutenant Dixon readily procured a volunteer crew, his little vessel was fitted with a Lee spar torpedo, and the expedition was undertaken. Lieutenant Dixon, acting with characteristic coolness and resolution, struck and sunk the *Housatonic* on the night of February 17, 1864; but unhappily, from some unknown cause, the torpedo boat was also sunk, and all with it lost. Several years since a "diver," examining the wreck of the *Housatonic*, discovered the fish-boat lying alongside of its victim.

From the commencement of the siege of Charleston I had been decidedly of the opinion that the most effective as well as least costly method of defense against the powerful iron-clad steamers and monitors originated during the late war, was to use against them small but swift steamers of light draught, very low decks, and hulls iron-claded down several feet below the water-line; these boats to be armed with a spar-torpedo (on Captain Lee's plan), to thrust out from the bow at the moment of collision, being inclined to strike below the enemy's armor, and so arranged that the torpedo could be immediately renewed from within for another attack; all such boats to be painted gray like the blockade-runners, and, when employed, to burn anthracite coal, so as to make no smoke. But unfortunately, I had not the means to put the system into execution. Soon after the first torpedo attack, made, as related, by the *David* upon the *New Ironsides*, I caused a number of boats and barges to be armed with spar-torpedoes for the purpose of attacking in detail the enemy's gunboats resorting to the sounds and harbors along the South Carolina coast. But, the Federals having become very watchful, surrounded their steamers at night with nettings and floating booms to prevent the torpedo boats from coming near enough to do them any injury. Even in the outer harbor of Charleston, where the blockaders and their consorts were at anchor, the same precaution was observed in clam weather.

The anchoring of the large torpedoes in position was attended with considerable danger. While planting them at the mouth of the Cooper and Ashley rivers (which form the peninsula of the city of Charleston), the steamer engaged in that duty being swung around by the returning tide, struck and exploded one of the torpedoes just anchored. The steamer sank immediately, but, fortunately, the tide being low and the depth of water not great, no lives were lost. In 1863-4, Jacksonville, Florida, having been evacuated by the Confederates, then too weak to hold it longer, the Federal gunboats frequently ran up the St. John's river many miles, committing depredations along its banks. To stop these proceedings I sent a party from Charleston under a staff officer, Captain Pliny Bryan, to plant torpedoes in the channels of that stream. The result was the destruction of several large steamers and cessation of all annoyance on the part of the others. In the bay of Charleston and adjacent streams I had planted about one hundred and twenty-five torpedoes and some fifty more in other parts of my department. The first torpedoes used in the late war were placed in the James river, below Richmond, by General G. R. Raines, who became afterward chief of the Torpedo Bureau. Mr. Barbarin, of New Orleans, placed also successfully a large number of torpedoes in Mobile bay and its vicinity.

To show the important results obtained by the use of torpedoes by the Confederates and the importance attached, now, at the North to that mode of warfare, I will quote here the following remarks from an able article in the last September number of the Galaxy, entitled, "Has the Day of Great Navies Past?" The author says: "The real application of submarine warfare dates from the efforts of the Confederates during the late war. In October, 1862, a 'torpedo bureau' was established at Richmond, which made rapid progress in the construction and operations of these weapons until the close of the war in 1865. Seven Union ironclads, eleven wooden war vessels, and six army transports were destroyed by Southern torpedoes, and many more were seriously damaged. This destruction occurred, for the most part, during the last two years of the war, and it is suggestive to think what might have been the influence on the Union cause if the Confederate practice of submarine warfare had been nearly as efficient at the commencement as it was at the close of the war. It is not too much to say, respecting the blockade of the Southern ports, that if not altogether broken up, it would have been rendered so inefficient as to have command no respect from European powers, while the command of rivers, all important to the Union forces as bases of operations, would have been next to impossible."

"Think of the destruction this infernal machine effected, and bear in mind its use came to be fairly understood, and some system introduced into its arrangement, only during the last part of the war. During a period when scarcely any vessels were lost, and very few severely damaged by the most powerful guns then employed in actual war, we find this long list of disasters from the use of this new and, in the beginning, much despised comer into the arena of naval warfare. But it required just such a record as this to arouse naval officers to ask themselves the question, 'Is not the day of great navies gone forever?' If such comparatively rude and improvised torpedoes made use of by the Confederates caused such damage and spread such terror among the Union fleet, what will be the consequence when skillful engineers, encouraged by governments, as they have never been before, diligently apply themselves to the perfecting of this terrible weapon? The successes of Confederates have made the torpedo, which before was looked on with loathing—a name not to be spoken except contemptuously—a recognized factor in modern naval warfare. On all sides we see the greatest activity in improving it."

I shall now refer briefly to the use in Charleston harbor of rifle-cannon and iron-clad floating and land batteries. In the attack on Fort Sumter, in 1861, these war appliances were first used in the United States. When I arrived at Charleston, in March of that year, to assume command of the forces there assembling and direct the attack on Fort Sumter, I found under construction a rough floating battery made of palmetto logs, under the direction of Captain Hamilton, an ex-United States naval officer. He intended to plate it with several sheets of rolled iron, each about three-quarters of an inch thick, and to arm it with four 32-pounder carronades. He and his battery were so much ridiculed, however, by the State government. He came to me in great discouragement, and expressed in vivid terms his certainty of success, and of revolutionizing future naval warfare as well as the construction of war vessels. I approved of Captain Hamilton's design, and having secured the necessary means, instructed him to finish his battery at the earliest moment practicable. This being accomplished before the attack on Fort Sumter opened, early in April I placed the floating battery in position at the western extremity of Sullivan's Island to enfilade certain barbette guns of the fort which could not be reached effectively by our land batteries. It therefore played an important part in that brief drama of thirty-three hours, receiving many shots without any serious injury. About one year later, in Hampton Roads, the *Virginia*, plated and roofed with two layers of railroad iron, met the *Monitor* in a momentous encounter, which first attracted the attention of the civilized world to the important change that iron-plating or "armors" would thenceforth create in naval architecture and armaments. The one and a half to two-inch plating used on Captain Hamilton's floating battery has already grown to about twelve inches thickness of steel plates of the best quality, but together with the utmost care, in the effort to resist the heaviest rifle-shots now used. About the same time that Captain Hamilton was constructing his floating battery, Mr. C. H. Steven, of Charleston, (who afterward died a brigadier-general at the battle of Chickamauga), commenced building an iron-clad land battery at Cumming's Point, the northern extremity of Morris Island and the point nearest to Fort Sumter—that is, about thirteen hundred years distant. This battery was to be built of heavy timbers covered with one layer of railroad iron, the rails well-fitted into each other, presenting an inclined, smooth surface of about thirty-fire degrees to the fire of Sumter; the surface was to be well greased and the guns were to fire through small embrasures supplied with strong iron shutters. I approved also of the plan, making such suggestions as my experience as an engineer warranted. This battery took an active part in the attack and was struck several times; but excepting the jamming and disabling one of the shutters, the battery remained uninjured to the end of the fight.

From Cumming's Point also, and in the same attack, was used the first rifled cannon fired in America. The day before I received orders from the Confederate Government, at Montgomery, to demand the evacuation or surrender of Fort Sumter, a vessel from England arriving in the outer harbor, signaled that she had something important for the Governor of the State. I sent out a harbor boat, which returned with a small Blakely rifled-gun, of two and a half inches diameter, with only fifty rounds of ammunition. I placed it at once behind a sand-bag parapet next to the Steven battery, where it did opportune service with its ten-pound shell while the ammunition lasted. The penetration of the projectiles into the brick masonry of the fort was not great at that distance, but the piece had great accuracy, and several of the shells entered the embrasures facing Morris Island. One of the officers of the garrison remarked after the surrender, that when they first heard the singular whizzing, screeching sound of the projectile, they did not understand its cause until one of the unexploded shells being found in the fort the mystery was solved. As a proof of the rapid strides taken by the artillery arm of the service, I shall mention that two years later the Federals fired against Fort Sumter, from nearly the same spot, rifle projectiles weighing three hundred pounds. Meantime I had received from England two other Blakely rifled cannon of thirteen and a quarter inches calibre. These magnificent specimens of heavy ordnance were, apart from their immense size, different in construction from any thing I had ever seen. They had been bored through from muzzle to breech; the breech was then plugged with a brass block extending into the bore at least two feet, and into which had been reamed a chamber about eighteen inches in length and six in diameter, while the vent entered the bore immediately in advance of this chamber. The projectiles provided were shells weighing, when loaded, about three hundred and fifty pounds, and solid cylindrical shots weighing seven hundred and thirty pounds; the charge for the latter was sixty pounds of powder. The first of these guns received was mounted in a battery specially constructed for it at "The Battery," at the immediate mouth of Cooper river, to command the inner harbor. As no instructions for their service accompanied the guns, and the metal between the exterior surface of the breech and the rear of the inner chamber did not exceed six to eight inches, against all experience in ordnance, apprehensions were excited that the gun would burst in firing with so large a charge and such weight of projectile. Under the circumstances it was determined to charge it with an empty shell and the minimum of powder necessary to move it; the charge was divided in two cartridges, one to fit the small rear chamber and the other the main bore. The gun was fired by means of a long lanyard from the bomb-proof attached to the battery; and, as apprehended it burst at the first fire, even with the relatively small charge used; the brass plug was found started back at least the sixteenth of an inch, splitting the breech with three of four cracks and rendering it useless.

With such a result I did not attempt, of course, to mount and use the other, but assembled a board of officers to study the principle that might be involved in the peculiar construction, and to make experiments generally with ordnance. The happy results of the extensive experiments made by this board with many guns of different caliber, including muskets, and last of all with the other Blakely, was that if the cartridge were not pressed down to the bottom of the bore of a gun, and a space were thus left in rear of the charge, as great a velocity could be imparted to the projectile with a much smaller charge and the gun was subject to less abrupt strain from the explosion, because this air-chamber, affording certain room for the expansion of the gases, gave time for the inertia of the heavy mass of the projectile to be overcome before the full explosion of the charge, and opportunity was also give for the ignition of the entire charge, so that no powder was wasted as in ordinary gunnery. When this was discovered the remaining Blakely was tried from a skid, without any cartridge in the rear chamber. It fired both projectiles, shell and solid shot, with complete success, notwithstanding the small amount of metal at the extremity of the breech. I at once utilized this discovery. We had a number of 8-inch Columbiads (remaining in Charleston after the capture of Sumter in 1861) which contained a powder-chamber of smaller diameter than the caliber of the gun. The vent in rear of this powder-chambers, leaving the latter to serve as an air-chamber, as in our use of the Blakely gun. They were then rifled and banded, and thus turned into admirable guns, which were effectively employed against the Federal iron-clads. I am surprised that the new principle adapted to these guns has not been used for the heavy ordnance of the present day, as it would secure great economy in weight and cost. The injured Blakely gun was subsequently thoroughly repaired, and made as efficient as when first received.

In the year 1854, while in charge as engineer of the fortifications of Louisiana, I attended a target practice with heavy guns by the garrison of Fort Jackson, on the Mississippi river, the object fired at being a hogshead floating with the current at the rate of about four and a half miles an hour. I was struck with the defaults of trailing or traversing the guns—42-pounders and 8-inch Columbiads—and with the consequent inaccuracy of the firing. Reflecting upon the matter, I devised soon afterward a simple method of overcoming the difficulty by the application of a "rack and lever" to the wheels of the chassis of the guns; and I sent drawings of the improvement to the Chief of Engineers,

General Totten, who referred them, with his approval, to the Chief of Ordnance. In the course of a few weeks the latter informed me that his department had not yet noticed any great obstacle in traversing guns on moving objects, and therefore declined to adopt my invention. When charged in 1861 with the Confederate attack on Fort Sumter, I described this device to several of my engineer and artillery officers; but before I could have it applied I was ordered to Virginia to assume command of the Confederate force then assembling at Manassas. Afterward, on my return to Charleston in 1862, one of my artillery officers, Lieutenant-Colonel Yates, an intelligent and zealous soldier, applied this principle (modified, however) to one of the heavy guns in the harbor with such satisfactory results that I gave him orders to apply it is rapidly as possible to all guns of that class which we then had mounted. By April 6, 1863, when Admiral Dupont made his attack on Fort Sumter with seven monitors, the *New Ironsides*, several gunboats and mortal boats, our heaviest pieces had this traversing apparatus adapted to their chassis, and the result realized fully our expectations. However slow or fast the Federal vessels moved in their evolutions, they received a steady and unerring fire, which at first disconcerted them, and at last gave us a brilliant victory—disabling fire of the monitors, one of which, the *Keokuk*, sunk at her anchors that night. It is pertinent for me professionally to remark that had this Federal naval attack on Fort Sumter of the 6th of April, 1863, been made at night, while the fleet could have easily approached near enough to see the fort—a large, lofty object, covering several acres—the monitors, which were relatively so small and low on the water, could not have been seen from the fort. It would have been impossible, therefore, for the latter to have returned with any accuracy the fire of the fleet, and this plan of attack could have crumbled under the enormous missiles, which made holes two and a half feet deep in the walls, and shattered the latter in an alarming manner. I could not then have repaired during the day the damages of the night, and I am confident now, as I was then, that Fort Sumter, if thus attacked, must have been disabled and silenced in a few days. Such a result at that time would have been necessarily followed by the evacuation of Morris and Sullivan's Islands, and, soon after, of Charleston itself, for I had not yet had time to complete and arm the system of works, including James Island and the inner harbor, which enabled us six months later to bid defiance to Admiral Dahlgren's powerful fleet and Gilmore's strong land forces.

Appendix G

How the *Hunley* was Found

(The story that appeared in *Blue & Gray Magazine*—vol. XIII, issue 5)

The Search for the *Hunley*
A Twenty Three Year Mission Ends in Success.
By
Christopher Chase

The story of the CSS *H. L. Hunley* has been well told in books and the popular press. Untold, until now, are the details of the early search for the submarine by the Sons of Confederate Veterans organization, and the information that led to its discovery.

Throughout most of the 131 years since the *Hunley* failed to return home from its historic mission, authorities assumed it had sunk with its victim, the Federal blockade ship USS *Housatonic*. In 1973 writer/researcher Mark Newell chose to believe otherwise, accepting at face value the report of a Confederate officer who stated that he had exchanged pre-arranged signals with the submarine some time after the attack. Lieutenant Colonel O. M. Danztler reported from Head-quarters, Battery Marshall on February 17th, 1864, "The signals agreed upon to be given in case the boat wished a light to be exposed at this post as a guide for its return were observed and answered."

At the time there was no independent confirmation of this exchange of signals. Confederate States Army Captain Gray of the Office of Submarine Defenses appeared to be unaware of Danztler's report. In April of that same year, he advised Major-General Maury, "I am of the opinion that she went into the hole made in the *Housatonic* by the explosion of torpedoes and did not have sufficient power to back out."

Both these reports led to misconceptions on the part of future historians and researchers. Many assumed that Dantzler's language meant that the submarine wished to be guided back to Breach Inlet by the signal light. Others assumed that Gray's opinion was valid, and that the submarine did in fact sink with its victim and was scrapped when the wreckage of the *Housatonic* was salvaged after the war.

Newell's decision to rely on Dantzler's report was confirmed as correct when some years later archival research revealed the records of the Court of Inquiry into the sinking of the *Housatonic*. The eyewitness accounts of the survivors clearly confirmed that the *Hunley* left the scene of the attack. Some time later signal lights were observed being exchanged between a point in the ocean and another on Sullivan's Island. These facts were first published in Kleoppel's book *Danger Beneath the Waves* in 1987.

In 1972, Newell brought his conclusions to the head of the Sons of Confederate Veterans in South Carolina. He joined forces with the SCV to begin what was to be a 23 year search for the submarine with the aim of recovering it and providing an honorable burial for its gallant crew.

Simple observation led Newell to the probable location of the submarine in 1973. It is known that Lt. George Dixon took his submarine out of Breach Inlet each time he launched an attack on the blockade fleet. The reason is obvious enough even today. As the tides begin to turn from slack to ebb in the Back Bay behind Sullivan's Island, a huge volume of water forces its way through Breach Inlet. The strong current must have provided a free ride to the crew of eight who sat behind Dixon at a hand crank used to propel the craft.

As the tides turn again to flood, the incoming current is not as strong. Clearly the Back Bay filled from other sources that provided the incoming tide with readier access. The obvious next choice was the huge entrance to Charleston Harbor on the south end of Sullivan's Island. In escaping the scene of the attack, the crew of the *Hunley* would have taken full advantage of their knowledge of local tides.

Newell believed that Dixon signaled Battery Marshall from a location along a route from the wreck of the *Housatonic* to Charleston Harbor mouth where the strongest tidal flow would have lent speed to their escape.

The route led to Maffitt's Channel, which was closed in 1880 when massive granite jetties were built to aid navigation. Dives made in the area proved that the channel had silted in. These conditions meant that the area had to be searched with sensitive ship-towed metal detectors if the *Hunley* was to be found.

After several abortive attempts, this was accomplished in the summer of 1994, when Newell succeeded in encouraging author Clive Cussler to support a search of the area. Cussler had made brief and unsuccessful searches in 1980 and 1981 for the submarine. By 1994, Newell was completing a Ph.D. in underwater archaeology at St. Andrews University in Scotland.

The project searched almost fifty square miles of ocean off Charleston Harbor mouth in the first weeks of August, 1994. In the last days of the field work, an object matching the size and mass of the *Hunley* was found in the spot Newell had predicted, in the approaches to Maffitt's Channel, one of several 'targets' found in the general area.

A day was spent in September of 1994 carefully probing and mapping the object with volunteers who were able to determine that the object was within 30 to 40 feet long, within five feet wide and had a curved upper surface. Newell had been authorized by the Federal Government to dig small test pits in order to uncover and hopefully identify any objects found during the search. Rather than prematurely disturb a possible national treasure, Newell decided to examine the object with high resolution sonar in the Spring of 1995.

The time consuming conduct of such non-invasive science evidently tested the patience of the University's partner. In May of 1995, a month before sonar testing was scheduled, Clive Cussler ordered his own divers to excavate targets found in Maffitt's Channel area, revealing the *Hunley*.

Clearly, Cussler's intention was to pre-empt Newell's confirmation of the discovery and reap the benefits of the publicity for himself alone. Evidently, the theory developed in 1973 was correct. Once Dixon had rammed the *Hunley* into the side of the *Housatonic*, his crew reversed the submarine, unreeling the lanyard attached to the trigger on their 90-pound torpedo. When the line played out, it triggered the explosion with devastating effect. As the witnesses in the rigging of the *Housatonic* confirmed, the *Hunley* continued to back away. At some point, Dixon would have turned the bow to shore. According to his usual plan, the attack was timed for the change of tides.

As the crew of the submarine cranked for their lives to escape a counter attack from other Federal ships, the flood tide would have sped their way into Maffitt's Channel and the main harbor mouth. Dixon had arranged to give a signal to Battery Marshall to confirm that he had survived the attack. These were the lights observed by the survivors in the rigging of the *Housatonic* some 45 minutes after the sinking.

With the *Hunley* safely on its way home—what could have happened to send it to the bottom so close to the completion of its mission? This is the last detail to remain a mystery, one that will most likely be solved when the submarine is closely examined.

Two of the three crews lost in the *Hunley* during its trials in Charleston Harbor were drowned when accidents caused sea water to wash over the open hatches. To signal Battery Marshall from the submarine, Dixon would have to have opened the forward hatch to extend a carbide gas lantern. Those same big ocean waves that buffeted Newell as he hovered over the *Hunley's* grave in 1994, might also have been the cause of its final sinking. With perilously little positive buoyancy, the submarine most likely was swamped as Dixon was completing the exchange of signals.

We do know now that it came to rest on the coarse gravels of Maffitt's Channel with a slight list to starboard. The bow, carrying the iron rod on which the torpedo had been mounted (the pine spar had been removed a few days before the last mission) pointed toward the south end of Sullivan's Island less than a mile away. They were that close to home, safety—and a very different ending in the story of The War Between the States.

CHAPTER 1
THE *PIONEER*

1. ———, *Official Records of the Union and Confederate Navies in the War of the Rebellion* (Washington, D.C.: Government Printing Office, 1884–1927), ser. 1, vol. 5, p. 796.

2. J. Thomas Scharf, *History of the Confederate States Navy* (New York: Crown Publishers, Inc., 1877), p. 54.

3. Ibid., p. 91.

4. ORN, ser. 1, vol. 1, p. 336.

5. F. G. Smith, "Submarine Warfare," *Mobile Advisor and Register*, June 26, 1861.

6. James R. McClintock, letter to Matthew Maury, Matthew Maury Papers, Washington: Library of Congress, Manuscript Division, vol. 46, items 9087–9094.

7. Ruth H. Duncan, *The Captain and the Submarine* (Memphis: S.C. Tool & Company, 1965), p. 53.

8. Ibid., p. 58.

9. Richard Wills, *The H. L. Hunley in Historical Context* (Washington: Naval Historical Center, 1998), p. 6.

10. McClintock, letter to Matthew Maury.

11. ORN, ser. 2, vol. 1, pp. 399–400.

12. Theodore Roscoe, *Picture History of the U.S. Navy* (New York: Charles Scribner's Sons, 1956), plate 739.

13. G. W. Baird, "Submarine Torpedo Boats," *Journal of American Societies of Naval Engineers*, vol. 14, issue 3, 1902, pp. 845–55.

14. William A. Alexander, "Thrilling Chapter in the History of the Confederate States Navy, Work of Submarine Boats," *Southern Historical Society Papers*, vol. 30, 1902, p. 165.

15. Mark K. Ragan, *The Hunley: Submarines, Sacrifice, & Success in the Civil War* (Charleston: Narwhal Press, Inc., 1995), p. 21.

16. William M. Robinson, Jr., *The Confederate Privateers* (Columbia: University of South Carolina Press, 1928), pp. 172–74.

17. Wills, p. 8.

18. James E. Kloeppel, *Danger Beneath the Waves* (Orangeburg: Sandlapper Publishing Co., 1987), pp. 9–19.

CHAPTER 2
THE *AMERICAN DIVER*

1. Mark K. Ragan, *The Hunley: Submarines, Sacrifice, & Success in the Civil War* (Charleston: Narwhal Press, Inc., 1995), p. 22.

2. ———, *Official Records of the Union and Confederate Navies in the War of the Rebellion* (Washington, D.C.: Government Printing Office, 1884–1927), ser. 1, vol. 15, p. 229.

3. James R. McClintock, letter to Matthew Maury, Matthew Maury Papers, Washington: Library of Congress, Manuscript Division, vol. 46, items 9087–9094.

4. Richard Wills, *The Hunley in Historical Context* (Washington: Naval Historical Center, 1998), pp. 4–9.

5. Franklin Buchanan, Letterbook, Chapel Hill: University of North Carolina.

6. ———, "Treasury of Early Submarines, " Annapolis: *U.S. Naval Institute Proceedings*, May 1967, p. 102.

7. McClintock, letter to Maury.

8. Buchanan, Letterbook.

9. William A. Alexander, "Thrilling Chapter in the History of the Confederate States Navy, Work of Submarine Boats," *Southern Historical Society Papers*, vol. 30, 1902, p. 165.

10. Buchanan, Letterbook.

CHAPTER 3
THE *HUNLEY* AT MOBILE

1. ———, *The War of the Rebellion, A Compilation of the Official Records of the Union and Confederate Armies* (Washington, D.C.: Government Printing Office, 1901), ser. 1, vol. 2, pp. 173–74.

2. Mark K. Ragan, *The Hunley: Submarines, Sacrifice, & Success in the Civil War* (Charleston: Narwhal Press Inc., 1995), p. 26.

3. William A. Alexander, "Thrilling Chapter in the History of the Confederate States Navy, Work of Submarine Boats," *Southern Historical Society Papers*, vol. 30, 1902, pp. 165–66.

4. Ragan, p. 28.

5. Ruth H. Duncan, *The Captain and the Submarine CSS H. L. Hunley* (Memphis: S. C. Tool & Company, 1965), p. 62.

6. Alexander, p. 166.

7. Richard Wills, *The H. L. Hunley in Historical Context* (Washington: Naval Historical Center, 1998), p. 11.

8. Ibid., pp. 166–67.

9. Ragan, p. 30.

10. Charles Lee Lewis, *Admiral Franklin Buchanan, Fearless Man of Action* (Baltimore: The Norman Remington Company, 1929), p. 212.

11. OR, ser. 1, vol. 28, pt. 2, p. 265.

12. Wills, pp. 13–14.

13. Ragan, p. 33.

CHAPTER 4
DISASTER AT CHARLESTON

1. James L. Nichols, *Confederate Engineers* (Tuscaloosa: Confederate Publishing Co., 1957), p. 68.
2. Mark K. Ragan, *The Hunley: Submarines, Sacrifice, & Success in the Civil War* (Charleston: Narwhal Press Inc., 1995), p. 35.
3. Ragan, p. 35.
4. Ibid., p. 38.
5. Ibid.
6. Ibid., p. 40.
7. James E. Kloeppel, *Danger Beneath the Waves* (Orangeburg: Sandlapper Publishing, Inc., 1987), pp. 32–34.
8. Ragan, p. 42.
9. Emma Holmes, *The Diary of Miss Emma Holmes, 1861–1866* (Baton Rouge: Louisiana State University Press, 1979), p. 236.
10. Kloeppel, pp. 37–38.
11. Ragan, p. 52.
12. W. R. Fort, "First Submarine in the Confederate Navy," *Confederate Veteran*, October 1918, p. 459.
13. Mark K. Ragan, *Union and Confederate Submarine Warfare in the Civil War* (Mason City: Savas Publishing, 1999), pp. 127–28.
14. Ragan, p. 54.
15. Henry Eichel, "Sub's First Crew Possibly Found," *The Charlotte Observer*, March 18, 1999.
16. Ibid., p. 56.
17. Ibid., p. 58.

CHAPTER 5
DISASTER STRIKES AGAIN

1. ———, National Archives, Confederate Records, letters received, record group, 109.
2. William A. Alexander, "Thrilling Chapter in the History of the Confederate States Navy, Work of Submarine Boats," *Southern Historical Society Papers*, vol. 30, 1902, p. 168.
3. ORN, ser. 1, vol. 15, p. 692.
4. P. G. T. Beauregard, "Torpedo Service in the Harbor and Water Defense of Charleston," *Southern Historical Society Papers*, April 1878, p. 153.
5. ORN, ser. 1, vol. 15, p. 693.
6. Beauregard, p. 153.
7. Alexander, pp. 168–70.
8. Ragan, pp. 73–74.

CHAPTER 6
DIXON TAKES COMMAND

1. James E. Kloeppel, *Danger Beneath the Waves* (Orangeburg: Sandlapper Publishing, Inc., 1987), p. 49.
2. Mark K. Ragan, *The Hunley: Submarines, Sacrifice, & Success in the Civil War* (Charleston: Narwhal Press Inc., 1995), p. 86.
3. William A. Alexander, "Thrilling Chapter in the History of the Confederate States Navy, Work of Submarine Boats," *Southern Historical Society Papers*, vol. 30, 1902, p. 170.
4. Ibid.

5. ORN, ser. 1, vol. 15, p. 337.

6. Kloeppel, p. 58.

7. ORN, ser. 1, vol. 15, p. 229.

8. ———, *The War of the Rebellion, A Compilation of the Official Records of the Union and Confederate Armies* (Washington, D.C.: Government Printing Office, 1901), ser. 1, vol. 28, pp. 553.

9. Ragan, pp. 96–106.

10. Ibid., p. 108.

11. Alexander, pp. 170–71.

CHAPTER 7
THE *HUNLEY* AT BREACH INLET

1. William A. Alexander, "The True Stories of the Confederate Submarine Boats," *New Orleans Picayune*, June 29, 1902.

2. Mark K. Ragan, *The Hunley: Submarines, Sacrifice, & Success in the Civil War* (Charleston: Narwhal Press Inc., 1995), pp. 114–20.

3. William A. Alexander, "Thrilling Chapter in the History of the Confederate States Navy, Work of Submarine Boats," *Southern Historical Society Papers*, vol. 30, 1902, pp. 171–72.

4. George E. Dixon, "Lieutenant Dixon's Last Letter," *Mobile Register*, March 14, 1900.

5. Alexander, "The True Stories..."

CHAPTER 8
THE *HUNLEY* ATTACKS!

1. ———, *Official Records of the Union and Confederate Navies in the War of the Rebellion* (Washington, D.C.: Government Printing Office, 1884–1927), ser. 2, vol. 1, p. 104.

2. J. N. Cordozo, *Reminiscences Charleston* (Charleston: Joseph Walker, 1866), pp. 124–25.

3. William A. Alexander, "The True Stories of the Confederate Submarine Boats," *New Orleans Picayune*, June 29, 1902.

4. ———, "South Carolina Confederate Twins," *Confederate Veteran*, Nashville: vol. 33, September 1925, p. 328.

5. ———, "Proceedings of the Naval Court of Inquiry," case #4345.

6. Ibid.

7. Alexander, "True Stories...."

8. ———, "Proceedings of the Naval Court of Inquiry."

9. Ibid.

10. Ibid.

11. Ibid.

12. Ibid.

13. Ibid.

14. Ibid.

15. Ibid.

16. ORN, ser. 1, vol. 15, p. 332.

17. ———, "Proceedings of the Naval Court of Inquiry."

CHAPTER 9
THE *HUNLEY* IS MISSING

1. ———, *Official Records of the Union and Confederate Navies in the War of the Rebellion* (Washington, D.C.: Government Printing Office, 1884–1927), ser. 1, vol. 15, p. 335.

2. Mark K. Ragan, *The Hunley: Submarines, Sacrifice, & Success in the Civil War* (Charleston: Narwhal Press Inc., 1995), p. 142.
3. Ibid.
4. ORN, ser. 1, vol. 15, p. 331.
5. Ragan, p. 144.
6. Ibid.
7. Ibid., pp. 337–38.
8. ORN, ser. 1, vol. 15, pp. 330–31.
9. William A. Alexander, "The True Stories of the Confederate Submarine Boats," *New Orleans Picayune*, June 29, 1902.
10. ORN, ser. 1, vol. 15, pp. 332–33.
11. Ragan, p. 154.
12. R. Thomas Campbell, "Gray Warriors Beneath the Waves—Update," *Confederate Veteran*, May–June 1993, pp. 10–13.
13. William A. Alexander, "Thrilling Chapter in the History of the Confederate States Navy, Work of Submarine Boats," *Southern Historical Society Papers*, vol. 30, 1902, p. 174.
14. R. Thomas Campbell, *Gray Thunder, Exploits of the Confederate States Navy* (Shippensburg: White Mane Publishing, Inc., 1996), p. 168.

CHAPTER 10
DISCOVERY

1. ———, "Remarkable Career of a Remarkable Craft," *Daily Republican*, October 8, 1870.
2. Mark K. Ragan, *The Hunley: Submarines, Sacrifice, & Success in the Civil War* (Charleston: Narwhal Press Inc., 1995), p. 170.
3. James E. Kloeppel, *Danger Beneath the Waves* (Orangeburg: Sandlapper Publishing, Inc., 1987), pp. 93–94.
4. E. Lee Spence, *Treasures of the Confederate Coast* (Charleston: Narwhal Press, Inc., 1995), pp. 44–45.
5. Ragan, pp. 179–80.
6. Christopher Chase, "In Search of the Hunley," *Blue & Gray Magazine*, vol. 13, issue 5, p. 26.
7. Clive Cussler, *The Sea Hunters* (New York: Pocket Star Books, 1996), pp. 218–19.
8. William Alexander, speech before the Iberville Historical Society, 1903.

Bibliography

_____. "Treasury of Early Submarines." Annapolis: *U.S. Naval Institute Proceedings*, May 1967.

_____. *The War of the Rebellion, A Compilation of the Official Records of the Union and Confederate Armies*. Washington, D.C.: Government Printing Office, 1901, ser. 1 vol. 2.

_____. National Archives, Confederate Records, letters received, record group, 109.

_____. "South Carolina Confederate Twins." *Confederate Veteran*. Nashville: vol. 33, September 1925.

_____. "Proceedings of the Naval Court of Inquiry," case #4345.

_____. "Remarkable Career of a Remarkable Craft." *Daily Republican*, October 8, 1870.

_____. *Civil War Naval Chronology*. Washington: Naval History Division, Navy Department, 1971.

———	*Official Records of the Union and Confederate Navies in the War of the Rebellion.* 31 volumes. Washington, D.C: Government Printing Office, 1884–1927.
Alexander, William A.	Speech before the Iberville Historical Society, 1903.
Alexander, William A.	"The True Stories of the Confederate Submarine Boats." *New Orleans Picayune*, June 29, 1902.
Alexander, William A.	"Thrilling Chapter in the History of the Confederate States Navy, Work of Submarine Boats." *Southern Historical Society Papers*, vol. 30, 1902.
Baird, G. W.	"Submarine Torpedo Boats." *Journal of American Societies of Naval Engineers*, vol. 14, issue 3, 1902.
Beauregard, P. G. T.	"Torpedo Service in the Harbor and Water Defense of Charleston." *Southern Historical Society Papers*, April 1878.
Buchanan, Franklin	Letterbook. Chapel Hill: University of North Carolina.
Burton, E. Milby	*The Siege of Charleston 1861-1865.* Columbia: University of South Carolina Press, 1970.
Campbell, R. Thomas	*Gray Thunder.* Shippensburg: White Mane Publishing Company, Inc., 1996.
Campbell, R. Thomas	"Gray Warriors Beneath the Waves—Update." *Confederate Veteran.* May–June 1993.
Chase, Christopher	"In Search of the Hunley." *Blue & Gray Magazine*, vol. 13, issue 5.
Cordozo, J. N.	*Reminiscences Charleston.* Charleston: Joseph Walker, 1866.
Coski, John M.	*Capital Navy.* Campbell: Savas Woodbury Publishers, 1996.
Current, Richard N.	*Encyclopedia of the Confederacy.* 4 volumes. New York: Simon & Schuster, 1993.
Cussler, Clive	*The Sea Hunters.* New York: Pocket Star Books, 1996.
Defour, Charles L.	*The Night the War was Lost.* Lincoln: University of Nebraska Press, 1960.

Dixon, George E.	"Lieutenant Dixon's Last Letter." *Mobile Register*, March 14, 1900.
Duncan, Ruth H.	*The Captain and the Submarine*. Memphis: S. C. Tool & Company, 1965.
Durkin, Joseph T.	*Confederate Navy Chief: Stephen R. Mallory*. Chapel Hill: The University of North Carolina Press, 1954.
Ford, Arthur P.	"The First Submarine Boat." *Confederate Veteran*, November 1908.
Fort, W. B.	"First Submarine in the Confederate Navy." *Confederate Veteran*, October, 1918.
Holmes, Emma	*The Diary of Miss Emma Holmes, 1861-1866*. Baton Rouge: Louisiana State University Press, 1979.
Johnson, John	*The Defense of Charleston Harbor*. Charleston: Walker, Evans & Cogswell Co., Publishers, 1890.
Jones, Virgil C.	*The Civil War at Sea*. 3 volumes. New York: Holt, Rinehart, and Winston, 1960–1962.
Kloeppel, James E.	*Danger Beneath the Waves*. Orangeburg: Sandlapper Publishing, Co., 1987.
Lewis, Charles Lee	*Admiral Franklin Buchanan, Fearless Man of Action*. Baltimore: The Norman Remington Company, 1929.
Luraghi, Raimondo	*History of the Confederate Navy*. Annapolis: Naval Institute Press, 1996.
McClintock, James R.	Letter to Matthew Maury, Matthew Maury Papers, Washington: Library of Congress, Manuscript Division, vol. 46, items 9087–9094.
Moebs, Thomas T.	*Confederate States Navy Research Guide*. Williamsburg: Moebs Publishing Company, 1991.
Nichols, James L.	*Confederate Engineers*. Tuscaloosa: Confederate Publishing Co., 1957.
Perry, Milton F.	*Infernal Machines*. Baton Rouge, Louisiana State University Press, 1965.
Ragan, Mark K.	*The Hunley: Submarines, Sacrifice, & Success in the Civil War*. Charleston: Narwhal Press, Inc., 1995.

Ragan, Mark K.   "Union and Confederate Submarine Warfare." *North & South Magazine,* vol. 2, no. 3.

Ragan, Mark K.   *Union and Confederate Submarine Warfare in the Civil War.* Mason City: Savas Publishing, 1999.

Ripley, Warren   *The Battery, Charleston, South Carolina.* Charleston: Post-Courier Booklet, 1877.

Robinson, William M. Jr.,   *The Confederate Privateers.* Columbia: University of South Carolina Press, 1928.

Roscoe, Theodore   *Picture History of the U.S. Navy.* New York: Charles Scribner's Sons, 1956.

Rosen, Robert N.   *Confederate Charleston.* Columbia: The University of South Carolina Press, 1994.

Schafer, Louis S.   *Confederate Underwater Warfare.* Jefferson: McFarland & Company, Inc., 1996.

Scharf, J. Thomas   *History of the Confederate States Navy.* New York: Crown Publishers, Inc., 1877.

Silverstone, Paul H.   *Warships of the Civil War Navies.* Annapolis: Naval Institute Press, 1989.

Smith, F. G.   "Submarine Warfare." *Mobile Advisor and Register,* June 26, 1861.

Spence, E. Lee   *Treasures of the Confederate Coast.* Charleston: Narwhal Press, Inc., 1995.

Stanton, C. L.   "Submarines and Torpedo Boats." *Confederate Veteran,* September 1914.

Stern, Philip Van Doren   *The Confederate Navy, A Pictorial History.* New York: Bonanza Books, 1962.

Still, William N.   *The Confederate Navy, The Ships, Men and Organization, 1861-65.* Annapolis: Naval Institute Press, 1997.

Wilcox, Arthur M.   *The Civil War at Charleston.* Charleston: Post-Courier Booklet, 1966.

Wills, Richard   *The H. L. Hunley in Historical Context.* Washington: Naval Historical Center, 1998.

Index

171